Sha Jackson was around the age of 10 when she had her initial encounter with molestation. It continued for a few years. *Booty Call* is her poignant memoir of how molestation, verbal abuse, weight problems, low self-esteem, and a failing marriage led her to an early life plagued with drug and alcohol abuse, sexual promiscuity and unplanned pregnancies. Sha found solace in her Lord and Savior Jesus Christ and was able to overcome those obstacles. She loves the Lord and knows He heard her cry.

Contents

Dedication

I would like to dedicate this book to Jesus, my Lord, to be used for your Glory. May you always be Glorified.

To my dear, sweet parents and to everyone in this world who struggles with the issues of life, this book is dedicated to you.

Acknowledgements

I thank my God, my Lord, Savior and my dearest friend, Jesus Christ, for saving me, for loving me, and for never leaving me nor forsaking me. I thank God for allowing my parents to live long enough to see that I really am a new person. I thank God for inspiring me and giving me the POWER to get this book in this earth.

I thank my dear mother for always praying for me and trying so hard to take care of me all of my life. She was such a wonderful woman. God honored my prayer and allowed her and dad to witness my deliverance for over twenty years, for which I am eternally grateful.

I thank you dad for always loving and providing for your family. I thank you for having the courage to stay in a home with five women. I also thank you for all of your words of wisdom and for everything that you have taught me.

I thank my dear, sweet sisters Sheila, Santa and Sharmel for forgiving me when I was totally out of control and for praying for me before, during and after my addiction. Your support, prayers, love and wisdom helped me get back on my feet once the storm was over. I thank God for the way our parents raised us. Nothing will ever be able to separate us. Last but not least, thank you for taking good care of my precious little children

I thank you Michael for continuing to be my husband. You have loved me unconditionally without fail more and more since the first day we met. You are my friend and my lover, always and forever! God has truly blessed us. The best is yet to come! Until Death Do Us Part!

I thank you Carol Whitton for helping to disciple me from 1987-1990. You were heaven sent and played a vital role in my life.

I thank you Pastor Montoya for calling me, without fail, every weekend to invite me to Sunday School while I was attending your church.

I thank you Pastor Gloria Leavell and the late Pastor Major Leavell of Holiness Church of Deliverance for being my spiritual leader for more than 20 years. Thank you for all of your teaching, love, correction and support.

I thank you Michael, Jr., my first and only son, for always being a pleasure to have as a child. You have never given me any trouble. I knew just a few days after you were born that you were going to be a wonderful child and you still are. Thank you for forgiving me for not always being a good mother and for my four beautiful grandchildren: Khallid, Michaela, Olivia and John Michael III. I love you son.

I thank you daughter, Shishonna, for being a beautiful miracle. Thank you for all of the lovely songs that were sung in the night. God has truly blessed you from the womb and I pray you continue to seek Him concerning your calling. Thank you for my three handsome grandsons: De'Shaun, Jaden and Demari.

I thank you my daughter-in-law, Yolonda, for my grandchildren and for taking such great care of my son. I thank the good Lord for our relationship. Continue to keep up the noble work and do mighty exploits for the Lord.

I thank you my grandchildren's fathers, Demarcus and Raphael. Thank you for being a father to your sons.

To my in-laws Mr. Clinton and Ms. Carrie thank you for your kindness.

To my Godchildren, Jovanna, Kiana, Leilani, Michaela, Naomi, and Josh, I never thought I would live this long to enjoy you all.

Thanks to all of you, especially my friend, Mrs. Ivory Warford, for encouraging me to finish my book.

I thank my boss, friend, and sister in Christ, Charlotte Moore, for encouraging me to seek employment where we currently work. You are always so gentle and kind.

I thank all my aunts, uncles, cousins, friends and extended family that prayed for me, believed in me and encouraged me. Your care, concern and labor of love will always be appreciated. Thank you for never giving up. This book is dedicated to you. Each of you has a special place in my heart and you know who you are! Many of you have helped my children and me in numerous ways. I thank you and I do remain mindful of your labor of love. There are so many of you I can't list you individually.

To April and Edwina, I thank you for allowing us to remain true friends for over 45 years.

I thank Elijah Davis II for drawing the beautiful rose and butterfly for me.

Lastly, I would like to acknowledge and especially thank a young lady for helping me put this project together. You are superlative, genuine, honest, true and most of all pure. I prayed for some help and God sent me the best angel he had. I will always love you, and you know who you are!

Hello my name Sha Jackson and I would like to tell my story…

Chapter 1
In the Beginning

Although it has taken me almost eight years to write this book, I can truly say, "I didn't give up and it is finished!"

Around the age of ten the molestation along with the verbal abuse began. Being such a young girl, I didn't know if I should tell, or who to tell. When I was instructed, "Shush! Don't say anything," I did just that. I was very quiet about the whole situation. I felt hurt, alone and afraid, but for some reason I suppressed my feelings and tried to live a normal life. I could go on as usual, only until it happened again. Because of the persistent gnawing on the inside, I knew I was going to tell my story, but I didn't know that it was going to be over forty years later! At that time I didn't know this was the beginning of a series of events that would ultimately led to my spiritual demise. Here is my story!

I am the second of four girls born to Melvina (B.B.) and Denoyis (Noy) in Los Angeles California. Out of all of us, I was the one who looked drastically different. I was very dark complexioned like my dad and all of the other girls were a caramel color like my mother. I had a weight problem from birth and I am knocked kneaded and pigeon toed. Because of the excess weight, I had trouble with my feet and had to wear corrective shoes. I also had very large breast at an early age. As a result of all of this I had troubles as an adolescent.

At a young age I began to notice that my family would always say things like, "She sure is dark skin, she sure is a fat little thing, and she looks just like her daddy." At that time, those words didn't hurt me too much because I was so young. I would wonder what in the world were they talking about. As I grew older though, I began to notice the significant difference and subconsciously began to wonder why being very dark and fat wasn't popular. I was teased and called names like "Black Sambo" and "Fatso." The older I got, the worse it became. I didn't feel very pretty and according to society, I wasn't. I felt fine about myself until someone reminded me of how different I was. Sad to say, all of the negative comments didn't come from the people outside of my family. It wasn't until I got older and started going to school that I really began to feel the pain in my heart. I was good at covering it up.

Unfortunately, I didn't have any brothers. I don't know how in the world my father managed all those years being the only male in the house with five women. Five women, can you imagine? He is a quiet man! He never talked a lot about his feelings but we knew by his everyday actions that he loved us and he cared. My daddy got up at the same time every morning and went to work until he retired. He is 85 years old and his memory is still very sharp! My mother was sort of a quiet woman too. She talked a little more than daddy did, but for the most part she was also quiet. They were a very nice couple and I knew they really loved each other because they were together until she went home to be with the Lord on August 29th, 2011.

I can remember sitting at the dinner table eating as a family and when I would ask for more food, my older sister would make a wise crack about my weight. She even told me that I would probably die of a heart attack because I had too much fat around my heart. Well, as a young girl I didn't understand this. I was just doing what I saw others do. I would eat all of the food on my plate as instructed, and if I was still hungry I would ask for seconds. I knew that I was heavy but to me, I wasn't that big. I wasn't a lazy person either. I would ride my bike, skate, and even run around the neighborhood with all of the other children. Some of them I could even out run. But for some reason the weight wouldn't come off.

For the most part, I had a wonderful childhood. For instance, my first day of school, there are parts of that day that I can remember like it was yesterday. My mother sat me on the edge of the bed and put on my school shoes. I was so excited about going to school. It was fun for me and I loved attending and making good grades in spite of the trouble and ridicule that I sustain. In addition to the teasing, boys would often times touch my breast and run. I wasn't having that! My daddy taught me that I didn't have to take it so I didn't.

My father taught us to be obedient and respectful. My dad also taught us not to start any fights but to always defend ourselves. If we had a problem with another child, we were to report it to the proper school officials. In other words, he said, "You better not start anything with anyone, but end it if that's what it takes," and I did just that. One day I wore a new dress to school sewn by my mother. She would sew a lot of my dresses because I was very top heavy. While in the 3rd or 4th grade during recess, I was playing baseball. I was on one of the bases and a boy ran by me and touched my breast. We began fighting and the yard teacher broke us up. While she was pulling us apart, I realized that he ripped my new dress. At that point, I grew even more furious and began beating on him again. Now I was in big trouble. I didn't care though. I felt he deserved it. He not only touched me but he had ripped the dress my momma made. I said all of that to say, this was the beginning of the water boiling on the inside of me!

In the 4th grade I was given an opportunity to play a school instrument and I chose to play the flute. I was already singing in the school choir. Playing the flute was a challenge, but I was determined to learn. I loved playing not only the flute but also any other instrument that I was taught to play.

I had a wonderful music teacher. Her name was Ms. Cox. I have never forgotten her name for some reason and I have a hard time remembering names. She was a very sophisticated lady. Not only did she know music, she was an excellent teacher. I can recall her telling us during choir; "Roll the tongue and use proper diction". I will never forget it and still cherish those memories. Because of the foundation that she laid for me during those years, I am still an avid music lover to this day. One day before class something awful happened.

A few boys in the front of the line outside of the music auditorium began horsing around. We were lined up single file waiting to get in. I was near the back of the line. They were going down the line poking fun at us. I was praying they wouldn't come and talk about me. At the same time, I was plotting my course of action. I was getting sick and tired of being picked on. I made up in my mind that as soon as he opened his mouth to say anything about me, I was going to rush him and beat him down. I was hoping they would finally open the door and let us in, but no, it was too late. He spoke about 2 words two me and I charged him so fast and hard, I don't believe he knew what hit him. I pushed him all the way to the front of the line, and slammed him into the building. I managed to get in a few punches and then he pushed me back and began to hit me. After that, all I can remember is getting hit in the eye. Fortunately, someone came and pulled us apart. That was probably a good thing because at that point I was having trouble seeing. I was taken to the nurse. After that incident I had to start wearing glasses.

Target

I began to notice boys and men were always coming on to me. It seemed as if someone was always trying to get into my panties. As a child I really didn't know what was going on and why these things kept happening to me.

One summer day, my mother sent me to the store to pick up a few things. For some reason I really didn't want to go to the store by myself that day. Needless to say I had to go anyway. The store was only a couple blocks away from my house. I decided to take a short cut through the schoolyard. I noticed the gate was open and I found this odd because I didn't see anyone in the schoolyard working. As I was nearing the other side of the school I still didn't see a soul. I was approaching the restroom and I decided to take a quick bathroom break.

This restroom wasn't unfamiliar to me. It was a really big bathroom containing about 20 stalls. I still had a funny feeling so I decided to check the bathroom out to make sure that no one was in there. Why did I have this feeling? I needed to hurry because my mother would begin wondering what was taking me so long. I Went into the stall and locked my door. Before I could pull my pants down, I heard someone walking very slowly down the front row of stalls. I could hear the sand on the ground crunching under their feet. I immediately began to panic and hold very still. I was praying that they wouldn't notice me, handle their business and leave. I held my breath so they couldn't hear me until I thought I was going to pass out. I even thought if I closed my eyes they wouldn't see me. I held my head down hoping that they would hurry up and walk on by. All of a sudden, I felt someone over my head. When I looked up, a man, or shall I say a teenaged boy was up there looking down at me. I thought I would die! I already knew what he was going to try and do. I was so scared I didn't want him to hurt me. I thought, "If he hurts me, how long would it be before someone found me in this bathroom?" On my God, what in the world was I going to do?

All of a sudden there he was, right in my face. He said, "Don't be scared, I'm not going to hurt you." Just him being right in front of me was hurting me! I was terrified as he started to gently put his arms around me and touch my face. All kinds of things were flowing through my head. I was whining, "No I can't do this, my mother is going to get me, and I am going to get in trouble." He told me, "Don't worry, no one is going to know. You won't get in trouble!" I pleaded, "Please don't, I know I will get in trouble, please, please let me go." I was really getting scared and I was getting aggressive because I wanted out. I was getting loud and because of the type of bathroom that it was, my voice was beginning to echo. I was struggling to get the bathroom stall opened. I managed to get free and I ran like a track star. I went straight home, totally forgetting about going to the store for my mother. I wasn't going to go back by myself. I didn't care what anyone said, I WASN'T going to go back! When I got home I told my mother what happened, and she looked like she was so hurt. She was just speechless. I went into my bedroom, fell on my bed, and I stayed there. I cried out, "Why me? Why me?"

Can't Even Go to the Movies in Peace

I remember I was about eleven or twelve years of age and my friends and I decided to go to the movies. It was a child appropriate movie so my mom gave us the okay. We were going during the day and decided to walk because it wasn't too far from the house. I believe it was my sister, two other girls, and I that went. We were all good friends and did almost everything together. We were having a good time as always. It was a beautiful day and we were laughing and talking all of the way there. Once we arrived at the show, the theater was practically empty. I mean ten people in the entire theatre. The Baldwin Hills Movie Theatre was a very popular place but it was a matinee and hardly anyone was there. We got our tickets and found a row of empty seats. The theatre became very dark as the movie began. We were sitting somewhat in the middle of the row and I was on the outside.

Suddenly, out of the corner of my eye I noticed someone had taken a seat at the end of our row. I kept watching the movie but the thought did cross my mind, "Why is this man sitting on this row with us when just about the whole theatre is empty?" As I continued watching the picture, I noticed him moving closer in the row towards me. I thought again, "Why is he moving closer?" Captivated by what was happening on the screen I tried to ignore him and what he was doing. All of a sudden he plopped right down next to me. At that point I started to get scared. I wondered, "What should I do? Should I tell someone what's going on? Why hasn't anyone else noticed this man?" As I continued to try to ignore him, I suddenly began to hear a strange noise. It was a sticky, sloshing, type of sound. I was petrified at this point. I didn't know if I should scream or what. I nudged my friend but she was too much into the movie to pay me any attention while I was being tortured. I began to ask God, "What in the world is going on?"

I decided that I would look and see what all of this noise was. Just about that time, he grabbed my hand and tried to get me to touch his penis. I screamed and ran out of the theatre. I told myself, "Run, run, run, as fast as you can, you better run! Run for your life, run girl run." I was a little chubby, but I could run fast especially when I was scared. As I was running I heard people calling me, "Sha, wait up, what is the matter? Sha wait for us! Wait." It wasn't until that time that I came to myself and I stopped running and I looked back only to find that he wasn't there. It was my sister and friends running after me.

I was crying profusely and was scared to death. I said to myself, "Why does this type of thing keep happening to me? What is wrong with me? Am I just a bad girl? Is that why all of these bad things keep happening to me?" When they finally got me to calm down I told them what just happened. They were upset and couldn't believe that a man came into the theatre and did such a thing. We went back to the theatre, the attendants took me inside to look for the man but he was gone.

I went home and told my mother. She asked, "What did you do?" I felt that I was being blamed for this. This was a real slap in the face. I was being violated and when I told someone about it, I was questioned as if it was my fault, or as if I had something to do with it. I couldn't understand how I could just sit in a movie theatre along with other people and be responsible for someone coming over to me and doing such a thing in public.

I asked myself numerous times, "Why me, why did and how could such a horrible thing happen to me? Why does this sort of thing keep happening to me over and over?" I was beginning to feel like I was walking around with a sign on my head saying "Violate me, I don't care."

Just Walking Home!

There was a time I was walking home down Labrea and this car sped down the street, pulled over and then stopped. This street is very busy and during that time of the day there was no parking or stopping allowed. I was wondering why he pulled over. As I began to pass his vehicle I glanced over only to find him exposed and stroking himself. I took off running all the way home. I couldn't believe he did this in the broad daylight. I was so scared, running and looking to see if he was following me home. Thank God he wasn't. This man was sick, and I don't know what his motive was, but again I felt bad that this happened to me once again. This stuff was beginning to make me angry. I remember telling my mother and she looked at me as if to say you poor little girl. She was a praying woman so I knew that she prayed for me! I'm just glad I didn't get hurt.

Even though he didn't physically harm me, just the fact that he showed himself to me in that fashion bothered me. Again, it left me with a lot of questions as to why this sort of thing kept happening to me. What in the world was I doing to deserve this type of treatment?

Unfortunately there were many other cases that are similar but these were mentioned because they are relevant to my story.

West Adams Foursquare Church

The thing that helped me cope with a lot of my adversity was going to church. One day this couple, Pastor Marvin and Juanita Smith, were walking door to door in our neighborhood inviting families to the church on the corner of Labrea and Adams Boulevard. My oldest sister asked my mom if she could take us there. I was amazed that my mother said okay because she was Catholic and attended St. Agatha church up the street. She didn't mind if we went to visit this church, which I ultimately became a member of and attended from age of four to eighteen.

I absolutely loved going to this church. We learned so much about Jesus and the Bible. What I liked most about West Adams was they had a lot of activities for children and they included us in almost everything. They believed strongly in teaching children. We were always taught what was right and wrong and how to witness to lost souls. We would have Sunday school, Bible drills, and our own choir called the L.S.T's for the teenagers. During the Holidays we would go Christmas caroling in different neighborhoods and to the convalescent homes. During the summer we had Vacation Bible School, Bible class, arts and crafts and would go to Disneyland, Magic Mountain, the beach, Mammoth Mountain, Yosemite, and many more adventurous places.

Our Pastors would invite us over to their house to go swimming. Sister Smith would always talk to us about how we should conduct ourselves as ladies in public. We were taught proper etiquette and how to cook. I must say, no one could cook or bake better than my mom and she always let us watch her too.

Despite the torture I sustained, I have to admit I had a wonderful childhood. In spite of all the bullying and ridicule that I had to sustain, I had a lot of good friends. I am still friends with two of my classmates from elementary school, one of which attended church with me. It's amazing, but we have kept in contact for over forty-five years.

Junior High School

After graduating from Cienega Elementary, I decided to go to Mount Vernon, Junior High School. I wanted to go to the same school my big sister had attended. I decided to continue playing the flute.

In my extra music class, the instructor taught us the basics of any instrument we wanted to learn. I learned how to play the drums, piano, trombone, bass drums, cello, violin and the bass. I can recall staying up at night to watch the Lawrence Welk Show and dreamed of someday playing in his orchestra. Meanwhile, I settled for the school orchestra where we took field trips to participate in competitions. It was very rewarding especially when we brought home the trophies.

The kids were not as cruel in Junior High School as they were in elementary school. Although I had grown a little taller and slimmer, I was still bigger than the majority of the other girls. Changing clothes in the gym was traumatic because the other girls would sometimes look at me and single me out. The physical fitness test was difficult because a lot of the exercises we were required to do, I couldn't do them, making me the joke of the day. After a while it all begins to take a toll on you, but for some reason, it wasn't as bad now as it was in elementary school.

New Boys in the Hood

In 1973 when I was a ninth grader, a man moved into the neighborhood. I found out he had five sons. My neighborhood friends and I would always look forward to meeting the new kids on the block. But this time it was a little different. No girls at all, just guys, and only one of them was our age. His name was David and he attended the same junior high school as I did. He was the baby boy and really cool. The oldest was away serving in the military and the next in line was away at college. All of the boys, or shall I say young men appeared to be nice. They would walk almost everywhere they went passing by my house.

Of course my sister and girlfriends from next door wanted to meet them. One day when the three amigos (that is what we would call them) were walking down the street, we hollered; "Hey, come over here and introduce yourselves." They did, and we were so excited. David was my age, but the other two brothers were too old for us to even think about getting with, so we were just excited to get to know them. We started liking these guys. Sometimes we would sit on my mother's front porch joking about which one we were going to try and catch for ourselves. The one I liked was Michael. He was four years older than me. He was the oldest of the three living at home with their father. I don't know why I was attracted to this guy because he was a lot different from all the other guys I knew. Sometimes we would yell, "Come on over and see us," but he would just smile and keep on walking. I could be in the house and see him coming or going and I would make my way out onto the porch. I knew when he passed by, I was going to say, "Hi", and he was going to throw his hand up in the air and give me the peace sign. As time passed, we became friends.

I do believe I was beginning to fall for this man, but to him, I was just a little girl that lived on the block.

Even though I was a size sixteen (that was considered big back then), men always wanted to see my breast. When people would talk to me, they would talk to my breast. To a young girl who still had her innocence, this was odd. As these strange things kept happening to me, I tried to stick to my plans. I had set some standards for myself; one of them was that the only man that would have pleasure in seeing my breasts would be my husband. I meant this with all of my heart. I wasn't going to be someone that men played with and tossed to the side. Besides, that's what I was taught in church, not to fornicate and to save myself for marriage. To my dismay, I was coming out of the little girl stage. Even more men were beginning to notice me, including Michael, the older brother that lived up the street. I no longer had to call to him, he would come and sit with me on his own. The next thing you know, we were dating. I felt so special to have a boyfriend who was much older than me. He was really my first serious relationship. Sometimes I would hear my classmates talk about how old he was. I couldn't believe it when he finally asked me out on a date, and surprisingly my mom allowed me to go.

He didn't have a car at the time, so we would catch the city bus to Hollywood. That's where we would go most of the time. I used to love walking down Hollywood Boulevard at night and on the weekends. We would see all types of crazy stuff. While we were in Hollywood, Michael would buy me little gifts. There were a large variety of novelty shops, so you could find anything you wanted. We would walk and hold hands going in and out of shops all night. There was never a dull moment in Hollywood, or like we used to call it back then, "Hollyweird!"

By the time the evening was over, I would return home with several little trinkets that I thought were so cute. Being the sweet boyfriend that he was, he would buy me whatever I wanted. He didn't have a lot of money to spend, but nonetheless, it was fun being spoiled by him. After we would stroll around for a while, we would catch the bus back home. He would walk me to the door and kiss me good night. That was all he was getting too, just a simple little kiss.

My mother would be waiting up for me on the couch in the dark, startling me the first few times she did this. I would go over and take a seat next to her and begin to share how the evening went, showing her all of the little things Michael purchased for me. I would tell her how we had such a good time just walking around, looking, spending a little money, talking and holding hands. Yes talking. I know that it might sound strange, but Michael wasn't like most guys. He didn't mind talking, laughing and joking around. As a matter of fact he was a happy go lucky kind of guy.

Michael was simply the fun, easygoing type. Even though he was older, we really had a lot of fun together. I believe I was infatuated with him. Most of the time he was really nice, kind and gentle. He really didn't have a lot of goals set. He was just living and enjoying life. He loved to go to the beach and he could swim like a fish, ultimately we courted there too. As much as I desired to go out in the water like he did, I couldn't swim. Michael would go so far out in the water until you could only see his little head. I, on the other hand, would only get my feet wet. At night we would sit on the rocks, watch the waves splash against the rocks and roll out again. The stars sat perfectly in the sky as the sun began to set displaying its array of different colors. It was beautiful watching the waves at night. I loved sitting there holding hands, talking and looking at the scenery. There's nothing like it. We really enjoyed doing that. Sometimes we would ride down the coast listening to music enjoying the ride. He loved to listen to hard rock and rock and roll. I believe his uniqueness is what attracted me to him. We had fun when we were together and that was all that mattered.

His dad didn't want us dating. I believe he felt that I was too young and he was afraid Michael would get me pregnant. But little did he know, at the time, pregnancy was impossible because I wasn't going to do anything that would enable me to get pregnant. Even though Michael was persistent in trying to sleep with me, it was to no avail. I had my mind made up. Sure, we would kiss a lot, but no hanky panky for me.

First Drink

One day, I went to visit Michael. His dad wasn't home so he offered me some chocolate liqueur. I was a good little church girl and I didn't drink nor did I smoke cigarettes or anything else. This wasn't the first time he offered this drink to me but for some reason, this day he convinced me. He told me it tasted like chocolate milk. After I tasted it, I thought it was pretty good. I only had a little that day. On a different day, but same scenario, he offered me a hit of a joint, or shall I say some marijuana. I had been resisting really well. I didn't want to smoke that stuff but I eventually gave in. I got so high I didn't know what to do with myself. Everything was so funny to me. It had started getting late and I knew that I needed to cook some rice before my mother got home from the laundromat (my parents owned a laundromat and Chinese laundry). I finally left his house and went home. While in the kitchen, I couldn't cook because I couldn't stop laughing. Everything was funny or funny looking. I remember going back to the front door and standing there looking out for my mom. I kept telling myself I was going to get in trouble if I didn't get in there and fix the rice but I couldn't move. When my mother pulled up, I was terrified but still laughing. I tried to stop but I couldn't. She was fussing about the rice but I didn't care because I was entirely too high. I went to my room and tried to stop laughing. She asked me, "What is wrong with you?" I don't know what I told her, but the first time I smoked a joint should have been my last, but it wasn't. Little did I know that it was just the beginning of a ride that I had no idea I was about to take! I know now, one thing will surely lead to another.

I was beginning to "backslide" as we call it in the church and I didn't even know it.

All of my morals and standards were being compromised. All of the things I told myself I would never do, I was beginning to do. All of the things I knew were wrong; I did them anyway, but with such conviction in my heart. I didn't know what danger I was putting myself in. I knew I should turn and walk away but the curiosity kept me coming back for more. After all, I was getting attention from a REAL man. Someone who was telling me that he really cared for me, he loved me, and I was beautiful. I just couldn't handle loosing that, so I thought anyway. I didn't see the trick of the enemy, or is it I really didn't want to see it?

Giving In

You can't keep playing with fire and not get burned. After about two years of Michael continuously asking me to have sex, I finally gave up my virginity, even though I really didn't want to. He said he would wait until we got married, but he really had no intentions on waiting. Because Michael told me he loved me and I knew I loved him, he convinced me it was the right time. He felt is was time for me to show him that I loved him and give up my precious virginity. So, I did! Michael decided we should go to his uncle's house one morning instead of me going to school. Skipping school wasn't something I did regularly. I took my schooling very serious, but against my better judgment, I skipped. The day I agreed to let him have my virginity, it took Michael hours to get it. I kept stopping him because I knew it was wrong and I was scared, and besides, it hurt! At this point, I really didn't want to continue with this but he wanted to. To be honest, I really wanted to wait for that special day, my wedding day, which was part of my plan. How much longer was I going to make him wait? Of course, he wasn't a virgin. He was very experienced and had all of the protection we needed, but that wasn't the way he wanted to do it. Michael convinced me to have unprotected sex and he assured me he knew what to do to keep me from getting pregnant. Because he was older and experienced, I listened to him despite all of the teaching I had received in health class and in church.

The day I gave in, I gave up! The whole ordeal wasn't fun nor was it enjoyable like people made it seem on television. It hurt so badly that for the next couple of days, I had a hard time walking. I was in excruciating pain. Who could I tell of this pain? I felt so alone! I was extremely disappointed in myself. This is not the way that I wanted to loose my virginity. It was my dream and goal to save myself for my husband on our wedding day. I often dreamed of what it would be like to give myself to my husband for the first time as a pure woman. I was determined I wasn't going to let different men in the name of a boyfriend have their way with me and then toss me to the side like an old blanket. I wasn't going to do it under any circumstances. I was so hurt and angry with myself, but the whole ordeal was irreversible. I couldn't undo what had already been done. A few days after we had sex, I healed and was okay. I told Michael he better not even think about having sex again and for a while he didn't. After I healed, there was endless sex between us.

Free Clinic

One day, my best friend, Nina, was going to the clinic to take a test because she thought she might be pregnant. She asked me if I would go with her for support. When we arrived at the clinic, there were a lot of people waiting to be seen so I was a little nervous sitting there. I didn't want her to leave me in the waiting room alone so we decided I should get tested too so I could be called back with her. Now, I knew I wasn't pregnant; I was just getting tested to kill time. To my surprise, when the results came back, we were both pregnant. I couldn't believe what I was being told. During this time, I was about sixteen years young and had my whole life ahead of me. I had lived a pretty sheltered life and I didn't have a clue as to what to do next. I was numb. We left the clinic speechless. I was devastated because having a baby right now would interfere with my plans for my life. A baby wasn't in the forecast, not now anyway. I sat there wondering what was I to do. This wasn't supposed to happen this way. Oh if I could make all of this go away. I felt I was living a nightmare and wanted to wake up. The reality was, this wasn't going to go away. This was really happening to me.

I was the one with all of the dreams and plans for my life. The one that supposedly had it all together. I was the little girl who knew who she was and where she was going. I was the one with so many standards and rules that were not to be broken. The one who always believed no one was going to get in her way. Just the thought of me blowing it, was unbearable. I felt I let everyone down.

What would my mother, my sisters, my friends, and the church say? My God, please help me! What would my father think of me? I didn't know if I would be able to face him. What would my boyfriend say? Would he stay with me or leave me? Especially now, after he has gotten what he had been trying to get for so long. So many questions I didn't have answers for. I looked at my friend and said, "Where are we going to tell our parents we've been for so long? It's so late and I know they're worried by now!"

When we reached the corner of Labrea and Westhaven, we rang the bell to get off the bus. Our stop to get off felt like my stop in life! It seemed my whole world had come to an end. Those were the thoughts that kept running through my head as we are walking to my mother's house, the house I hoped I would still be welcomed after I broke the news. I thought, "I am only sixteen; I am just a little girl. What in the world am I going to do?" My friend and I decided to tell our parents something stupid. I can't even remember what we came up with, but I do remember we agreed I wasn't going to say anything that night because I wasn't ready to tell my mom.

The door to the house was wide open. It looked like every light in the entire house was on. When we walked in, Nina's grandmother was they're looking for her. Because we were best friends and did a lot of things together, her grandmother immediately contacted my mother when she didn't come home on time. They knew we were probably together. Of course, the first words out of her grandmother's mouth were, "Nina! Where have you been?" I'm standing there saying to myself, "Remember what we said we were going to tell them." I am sure my face looked like I had just seen a ghost. Nina didn't stick to plan. I couldn't believe she started spilling her guts. She replied, "We went to the free clinic and I found out that I'm pregnant." I couldn't believe what was happening! Why didn't she stick with the plan? I had decided that I wasn't going to tell my mother, not just yet anyway. I was going to tell my boyfriend first, and then we were going to go together to tell everyone. All of a sudden, as Nina was talking, she said, "Sha is pregnant too!" At that point, I stopped talking to myself. My jaw dropped open in surprise and I looked directly at my mom. Not only did Nina deviate from the plan, but she also told my mother MY business. I knew at that moment I had better run and that's exactly what I did.

As I was running, my mother started yelling and chasing me around the dining room table. I screamed, "Momma! Momma! Momma, I'm sorry, I'm sorry! Please don't hit me! I'm sorry!" My mother grabbed this big belt. She wasn't playing. She was running after me like I had never seen her run before. She was really mad. I remember screaming and crying, "Momma stop, please stop, let me explain!" She continued to chase me. She was crying and yelling, "Oh God!" I couldn't take it anymore. I hated to see my mother hurting so much. I could tell by the sound of her voice and the look of disgust on her face, she was devastated! I ran in my room and fell on top of my bed. She ran in the room right behind me and began to hit me with the belt. I screamed because she was hitting me with buckle end of the belt. She didn't realize it was the buckle side. After she hit me a couple of times, she collapsed on top of my back and we laid there crying together. As we cried and cried, I kept telling her, "Momma, I'm sorry! I'm so sorry momma, I'm sorry!"

I lay there in a pool of tears and continuously apologized as my mother got up. I was afraid to move. I didn't know what was going to happen to me next. I don't remember what happened to Nina. I think they left.

My mom told me to call my boyfriend Michael and tell him to come to the house right away. I briefly told him on the phone what happened. He didn't hesitate. He came to the house immediately.

My dad entered the living room and sat down. I was sitting at the dining room table when Michael rang the doorbell. My mother answered the door and he came in and sat down in the living room. My mother began interrogating him. She was asking him what his plans were. Michael was so cool about everything, to the point that it got on my mothers nerves. She didn't like the way he was responding to her questions. I guess she took all she could take of him and his nonchalant responses. She started slapping him in the face and the head and telling him what he was and wasn't going to do. I was looking on in total shock because that was totally out of character for my mother. My parents were not violent people. I remember staring in suspense, waiting for my boyfriend's response.

As children, my dad would tell us stories about how he used to be a boxer. My father was very strong. I was afraid for my Michael because I knew if he flinched at my mother, my father would probably kill him with one hand. Thank God he didn't do anything but sit there and try to cover his head to block some of the blows my mother was throwing at him.

When my mother was finished talking and hitting Michael, she told him to leave and she slammed the front door. My father wanted me out of the house but my mother didn't want me to leave. She told me to get my things and go to my big sister's house, which was located directly behind my mother's house, and to stay with her until further notice.

I knew my big sister loved me, but I also knew how she felt about constantly having to take care of me and always having to drag me along. Now that she is out on her own, I knew she wouldn't want to be concerned with my problems. She was going to be upset because I had come, once again, to invade her space. I was afraid to go to her house. I just knew she was going to reject me. I hated being rejected, and when you have been rejected all of you life, you try to avoid it as much s possible. As I was standing there thinking about what I was going to have to face, I could hardly bear the thought of it. I was scared. My boyfriend had left me there all alone. Then, my father decided to get up out of the chair.

Up until this moment, he had not said a word to any of us. Again, my dad was a man of very few words, but when he spoke, every one listened and knew he meant business. I could tell by the look on his face he wasn't pleased with me at all. I could only imagine how he was feeling. I do know that when I would be rejected or misunderstood in the past, he would always be the one to understand me when no one else did. As he was approaching the dining room where I was standing, I felt like my life was a total disaster. I thought he was going to be my solace. Surely he would say something to console me. I remember saying to my self, "Here comes my daddy. I know he is hurt, but I believe he will say something to make me feel better." He was approaching, looking at me in silence and I was looking back at him in silence. He was getting closer and closer and yet, still not a saying a word. "Maybe he is going to take me in his arms and let me know that everything was going to be all right," I thought. He looked very angry, yet sad. As he opened up his mouth, he said, "Liar!" and kept on walking. With those words being said to me during my time of agony, he might as well as put a dagger through my heart. I knew I had really disappointed my father. I knew it! At that moment, my heart felt like it had burst and began to bleed uncontrollably. I felt worthless! I knew I had let everyone down.

Everyone believed me when I would speak of all of the things I wanted do in life. They had faith in me, but most importantly, I believed in myself. Am I a liar or did I just mess up? Was I a bad person? It was as if I could do no wrong in their eyes. I could make no mistakes. I had to always be right, but I was so wrong. I looked wrong, I walked wrong, and I was the wrong color, wrong shape and the wrong size. I was just wrong! Maybe for me to think so big of myself was wrong because now I was only sixteen, still in high school, single and pregnant!

I had really tried hard up until this point to do things right. My mom said to do well in school and I did very well all of the time. I loved learning and I was smart. Not a genius, but I was smart. If I set my mind to do something, I did it. I went to church and

I tried to live up to all I was being taught. I knew what a sin was and I tried not to sin towards God, but I also knew I was human and I would make mistakes sometimes. I did realize I had messed up big time. Why couldn't I just make him wait just a little while longer? Michael and I had talked about getting married. Why didn't I make him wait until he married me? Why?

I could stand there all night long and ask myself why, but it wasn't going to change anything. I wanted to run away, but I knew I had nowhere to go. Plus I was so scared. I felt like my life was now totally out of control. I felt like I couldn't even think for myself. Could I make the right decision about anything anymore? What went wrong for me? In an instant, life for me turned upside down. At least that is the way it felt.

"GET YOUR STUFF AND GO TO THE BACK HOUSE!" my mother yelled again. I had to snap out of it and get going. I didn't want her to go off on me a second time. I didn't want to have my older sister go off on me either. The thought of being rejected and all of the harsh words made me blank and numb. I began walking slowly, like a zombie, gathering my things, and left my mother's house. Before I went to my sister's, I went up the street to my boyfriend's house. I told him my mother had put me out and she wanted me to go and stay with my big sister. I told him I didn't want to stay with her. He told me I could stay with him in his room. The problem with that situation was, he was still staying at home with his father and other brothers, in a two-bedroom apartment. He was twenty years old, working, and still staying with his father.

We were lying across his bed talking when Michael's father came home from work that night. He went in to talk to him about us. His father told him that I couldn't stay there, and that he warned him not to mess around with me because he knew I was going to try and get myself pregnant. Again, I was the bad guy. I never wanted to give up my virginity. I wanted to wait until I was married. Michael was the one who always harassed me about having sex, but I bet he didn't tell his dad that. He let his dad believe I pressured him and got pregnant on purpose. He was the experienced one, not me. Michael told me he knew what to do so I wouldn't get pregnant. He had condoms but he told me that he didn't like the way they felt. I trusted him! I should have known better. We'll actually, I did know better but I didn't act on what I knew. I let myself believe that foolishness even though I knew better. People are going to believe whatever they want to believe even if it's a lie. It's as if no one ever tries to find out the truth, at least it feels that way! So I had to get out of his fathers house and leave. My boyfriend, to my surprise, was willing to take care of the baby and me. I was surprised he didn't reject me also. Maybe he really does care about me! Michael and

I left and walked slowly down the street to my big sisters house.

I knocked on the door and she let me in. I told her what happened. I can't remember her response except, she told me I had to sleep on the couch! I laid down and cried myself to sleep. When I woke up the next morning, I wanted to believe it was all a bad dream, but it wasn't. I stayed home all day. I didn't eat very much and I tried not to move too much either. I knew how my sister was about her things. I didn't want to make a mess. I made sure I cleaned up behind myself. But it really didn't matter what I did. Everyday when she came home from work she found something to complain about. I couldn't take it anymore. I had to go. I left and went back to my mom's house.

My mom had a long time to think about "MY" situation. After all, I was just sixteen and I was in the 11th grade. My mother's vision was for all of her girls to finish school and for us to make a good life for ourselves. Finishing school was going to happen for me no matter what, as far as I was concerned. Others felt I wouldn't be able to have the baby and continue my education. I didn't want to get rid of my baby, but I was numb, speechless and I felt that I couldn't make any decisions for myself. I felt like such a loser, and I didn't know anything. I told Michael how I felt. He didn't want me to have the abortion, but he didn't try too hard to stop me either.

I Killed my Baby

I was lying alone in this cool and dim looking room being prepped for an abortion. I said, "No I don't want to kill my baby, please don't kill my baby. I know that I can take care of her. I will finish school and become a nurse. We will get married and have a family. Everything will work out just fine. I know it will because I am good with children. Please don't make me do this. It is not right. Please don't make me do it!" No one was listening to me because they couldn't hear me. I was saying all of this to myself. I felt I didn't have a voice. I was doing a lot of talking, but I was only talking to myself. I remember the nurse saying they were finished. I rose up a little off the bed. I remember seeing a jar on a side table with what looked like a bloody mass in it. The nurse tried to get me to lay back down, but I saw it! I saw it and I couldn't reverse what I had just done. They didn't want me to see the jar with my baby inside. How in the world could I have killed my innocent baby? That wasn't a good thing for me to do. I began to feel faint. I felt like not only was I bad, useless, and a loser, but now I was a MURDERER!

At church we would always recite the Ten Commandments. The only one I could remember right now was, "Thou shall not kill" "Thou shall not kill." I had just killed my baby. Some how I just knew she was a baby girl and I had killed her. It is a wonder I didn't lose my mind that day! I remember crying everyday over the baby I had murdered. I told God that I was sorry, but being sorry didn't seem like it was good enough. "They made me do it. I didn't want to get rid of my baby, but I did. Lord I am so sorry," I said. "Nothing will ever bring her back. Nothing!" Even though I knew there was no way to bring my baby back, and I repented over and over and over again to God, my precious little baby was gone. I really missed that little baby. I thought about her all of the time. I just couldn't get her out of my mind!

I managed to continue to go to school and work. I was still dating Michael in my senior year of high school. I tried to go on like nothing ever happened but I must admit it was hard. Then one day something else that was very dear to my heart was stolen from me. I really wanted to play in the marching band but I was afraid they wouldn't be able to find a uniform big enough for me or it wouldn't look right on me. Fear wouldn't let me do it. I settled for the orchestra and was excited because my father had provided me with private lessons and he purchased me a Flute. One day, when I went to class, our regular music teacher wasn't there. The substitute teacher had never been there before. As far as the class period, it all went well until it was time to leave. The teacher wouldn't let me take my flute home. Everybody tried to tell him it was my personal flute but he still refused to let me take it home. Despite the fact I was furious, I had to go to my next class. I asked the substitute what he was going to do with my flute. He told me it would be locked up in the school safe and it would be fine. I left and went to my next class, but for some reason, it didn't set well with me. When I went home, the first thing I told my mother was what happened with my flute. She was just as upset as I was but what could we do? The next day, the regular music teacher was back. As soon as I walked in the room, he told us he had some bad news. He was looking at us really sad and serious. I knew at that instant, something had happened to my flute. Sure enough, he told us someone had broken into the school and had stolen a lot of instruments, and my flute was one them. I said, "WHAT?" I was floored! I tried to tell that man! If he had only let me take my instrument home, none of this would have happened. I was outraged! All I wanted to do was cry! I wanted to cry my heart out. Why was this happening to me? How was I going to explain this to my father? The teacher told me to go to the office and see what was going to be done about my flute. I hurried out of the room and went straight to the office fussing at myself about the situation. "I should have just taken my flute and ran out of the class yesterday and none of this would be happening right now" I said. When I got to the office, I was told to have a seat and someone would be right with me. Finally, I was called in the office and I was in tears. As I explained my situation to them, they quickly let me know the school did have insurance but it was only going to cover the instruments that belonged to the school and not mine. They said I should have had my own insurance on the flute. I couldn't believe what I was being told. I stormed out of the office and went to class. All the while I was saying to myself, "You just wait until I get home and tell my daddy! We'll see if you won't give me another flute."

Finally the day was over and I went home. I had to wait for my dad to get there, and when he did, I told him everything the school said. He looked at me and walked away. I asked him what he was he going to do and he said, "Nothing." "Nothing?" I said to myself. "What do you mean nothing? You aren't going to go to the school and make them give me another flute?"

I went to my mother and told her what happened. She looked at me and said, "Well!" "Well?" I said. "Nobody is going to do anything about this?" I went to my room and wondered if my dad was going to buy me another one. I really enjoyed playing the flute. I had been playing now for eight years. Playing and competition was a big part of my life. What was I suppose to do now? I was so hurt by the whole ordeal that I never played the flute again.

When I think about it now, I wonder why I didn't continue to play. I could have used the flute that belonged to the school and continued to play until I could get myself another one, but for some reason, I never play again. And yes, to this day, anytime I see someone playing the flute or when I listen to an orchestra, it takes me back to the days when I used to play.

High School Graduation

I had a lot of fun my last year of high school. Even though I wasn't playing in the orchestra, I was still in the PEP Club. The PEP Club girls were just like cheerleaders except we were in the stands. I loved being in the pep club. It didn't take the place of playing the flute but it would suffice. We went to all of the games and we had a ball cheering for the Dorsey Dons football team.

I was working and preparing to go to college. My counselor managed to find me a job at a nursing home to help me gain knowledge of my field of interest. I had a car and was back on track. I felt like I was able to retrieve myself. The people around me were beginning to believe in me again. They were even beginning to like Michael. He was like the brother our family never had. He was always around. Of course, I was put on birth control pills. They were going to make sure I didn't make the same mistake again. The only thing about the pills was, now I felt at liberty to have sex with Michael as much as I wanted to. At this point, I wasn't thinking about the fact that I was sinning and wasn't suppose to have sex outside of marriage (fornication), even if it was with a long time boyfriend who was promising to marry me. I guess at this point in my life it didn't matter. I was seventeen and I felt like I was on my way to being an adult and becoming my own woman.

I was still attending church and singing with L.S.T.s, "THE LORD'S SWEET TEENS." I really did enjoy going to church but I couldn't get Michael to go on a regular basis. Sure, a few times he did attend, but he didn't stay long. That should have been a sign to me then but I still wanted to be with him. I remember one day being at church and he came to get me. One of the ushers came in and told me that Michael wanted to see me. I got up and quietly tipped outside. I wondered what could possibly be going on that he would come get me out of church. To my surprise, when I stepped out onto the church steps, there he was drunk as a skunk. He was fussing and telling me to come and go with him. I immediately told him he needed to leave and go back home because I wasn't going to leave with him. I turned around and went back inside the church. I was so embarrassed for him and for myself. This was my boyfriend and everyone knew it. I was a little church girl dating a grown drunk man. How that must have looked, I really don't know, but I do know that it wasn't good. In spite of all we had been through, I still loved him and I liked being around him. Or was it just a "soul tie"? At this point in my life I really didn't want to know the truth. I just wanted us to continue to stay together.

On graduation night we were all so excited. I must admit I was a little nervous too. The graduation ceremony was held at the Hollywood Bowl in Hollywood, CA. If you knew anything about the Hollywood Bowl, you would say the same. The Bowl is the largest natural amphitheater in the United States. It is a place to go and enjoy beautiful music under the stars. It's a really nice place to have a graduation. Dorsey High School had the privilege of using the facility and had done so for many years. It was simply stunning. Walking across that big, beautiful stage in the bright lights was awesome. I didn't feel like a star, but I did feel like someone who had just completed a major accomplishment. I must admit, I was very proud of myself.

Twelve years of school and I had finally made it. This was truly a night to remember. I will never forget it as long as I live. I remember everything! It was Thursday, June10th, 1976. Wow! Words can't express the feeling I had. Everyone was so happy, parents and students alike. As they announced the class of "1976" we all jumped up and gave ourselves a shout of praise. "We did it!" I was excited and as far as I was concerned the night was still young. I was ready to go somewhere and do something. Have some fun; and hang out with friends.

After graduation, my family and I went back home. I thought I would get my clothes changed and go out with some friends, but my mother said I couldn't go. I asked repeatedly, "Why can't I go?"

All she said to me was, "Because I said so". I was shocked and I couldn't understand what was going on. Michael came over and she told me that I couldn't have any company. I told her it was Michael and he was like family and I couldn't understand why she wouldn't let me go any where with him or let him come in and talk to me. Any other time she didn't have a problem with me going anywhere with him. It's the night of my high school graduation! I don't know who I thought I was but I surely didn't think I was a little kid who had to go home after the ceremony. On this particular night when all of my friends were getting together to do something, I couldn't do anything. Not even with my boyfriend Michael who I always went out with. I remember looking at him though my bedroom window shaking my head and telling him, "I can't have any company." Since I was stuck in the house, I watched television and went to sleep. So much for being grown. I couldn't believe I had just graduated from High School and I had to stay home and go to bed.

Graduating from high school meant putting your money where your mouth was. It was now time to go on to college and pursue my dreams. I don't know why I didn't apply for a college scholarship. I always had good grades. I decided to start Los Angeles City College that summer. Some of my classes were hard, but I managed to get through them. Life was a little different now. College classes were not as easy as the high school classes. I began to struggle more. I wasn't used to struggling like this when it came to class work, but I was determined to succeed and not to fail. I gave it my all. There were many days I didn't like the hard work but I endured anyway.

I was determined to move on with my life, but I couldn't forget about my baby. The baby I had murdered through having an abortion. I missed her so much. We talked about it and Michael and I both agreed to have another baby. I didn't want to wait until we got married. I felt I could have a baby and finish college and we could get married later and life would be grand for us. I got pregnant again. I missed my baby so much! So this time, we didn't tell anyone we were pregnant. I wasn't going to let anyone take this baby from me. I kept working and going to school. My days were long. I would leave the house (Mom's house) early in the morning and I wouldn't make it home until late in the evening. Some days, I wouldn't get to see my mother at all. I was beginning to show and my clothes were getting tight. I told Michael I needed some clothes and he took me to Sears and bought me some maternity clothes.

We were trying to figure out how I was going to start wearing these clothes so no one would notice. I figured I would lay the clothes across the bed and some time during the day my mom would see them on the bed and she would get the hint I was pregnant. By not getting home until late at night, she would have time to make the discovery, get mad and calm down by the time I got there. When I finally got home, she asked me about the baby. I told her right away I was pregnant and I was going to have the baby. I told her I was going to finish school and I was going to marry Michael. She asked, "When are you going to get married?" I told her, "I don't know when but we are."

Chapter 3
Going to the Chapel

We'll I guess our plans to get married "some day" were not good enough. Before I knew it, we were arranging for a shotgun wedding. When Michael was asked about the wedding mom basically told him about the wedding. I went to the Pastor of my church and told him I was pregnant by my boyfriend and we wanted him to marry us. Without hesitation he informed me he couldn't and wouldn't marry us because Michael wasn't saved. We were unequally yoked and should not get married. He also informed me that because I was pregnant, I could no longer sing in the L.S.T.s. I loved to sing for the Lord and I loved our choir. With tears in my eyes and a broken heart, I asked him "Why." He told me "Because you are a teen going into womanhood you can no longer partake in any of the activities that pertained to the teens in the church."

I was crushed! Someone might as well have shot me right then and there! It seemed everything I really cared about was being taken from me. I knew I wasn't perfect, but I wasn't all that bad either. I was trying to do things right, well to some degree, but things kept going wrong. Really wrong! I made bad decisions and was trying to make them right, but to no avail. Why was everything going so wrong for me again? I just wanted to have my baby! I wanted someone to love me and return the love. Michael loved me and I loved him. He was the father of my unborn child so why couldn't we get married?

Because my church I had belonged to since I was about 4 years old refused to marry me, and because I was pregnant, it was suggested that we just go to Las Vegas and have a wedding in one of the little chapels. Michael agreed to go but this wasn't the wedding I wanted. I had always dreamed of having a big, beautiful church wedding. I didn't want to go to Las Vegas. I didn't like to gamble and that is all that they did there, so I thought anyway. I didn't like to drink and smoke and party. I didn't want to do any of those things.

After Michael and I agreed to the terms of going to Vegas, I told him, "You still need to ask my dad if you can have my hand in marriage." He did and my father said, "Yes." Michael proposed to me and my parents played a song for us so we could slow dance in the back room of the house. I will never forget that day. It was beautiful when he proposed, even though he didn't have the ring to put on my finger. A few days later, Michael took me to Hartman Jewelry on Washington Avenue in Los Angeles to get the ring. I saw this beautiful ring I liked. He told me to pick whichever one I wanted. I knew he didn't have a lot of money so I selected the smaller version of the design that I really liked, although I wanted the larger one. He insisted on the larger one but I told him we could get it later. He opened an account and we got the ring. He proposed again and put the ring on my finger. I remember thinking; "At least this part is right even though I didn't get the size I wanted."

I remember going to my anatomy class the next day and everyone was looking at my ring asking if I was engaged. I felt so proud as the ugly duckling (compared to my sisters) saying, "Yes, I am getting married!" And, I'm marrying an older man. I was only seventeen and he was now twenty-one. I met him when I was fourteen years old. First we were friends, then we became lovers, and now we were engaged to become man and wife and live happily ever after. To my friends, that was really something.

I agreed to go to Las Vegas and get married because I felt I had no other choice. My pastor refused to marry me! Everything was moving so fast. I could have inquired around town and found another church to have the wedding but because I was pregnant, I needed to do it and do it quick before I started to show. No big church wedding bells for me!

My parents rented a car and we all headed to Vegas, my older sister, her fiancé, my mom, Michael and I. My father wasn't planning to attend the wedding, but after arriving in Vegas, we were told he had to be there because of my age. My dad had to catch a flight to Vegas and attend the wedding after all. I am really glad that it happened that way, otherwise my daddy would have missed my wedding day and I would have been so disappointed. It is a day I will never forget as long as I live.

It was October 10, 1976, at the Little Chapel of the Flowers in Las Vegas, Nevada. I was pregnant and showing just a little bit. My dress was baby pink and I believe Michael wore the suit he purchased for my prom night. I remember sitting alone on the bench in the chapel foyer. My future brother-in-law came over to me and asked, "What are you thinking about?" I told him, "Nothing." He began talking to me and I just listened. I felt like it didn't matter what I was thinking or feeling so why bother to tell anyone. Again, I felt my dreams were shattered. Where were all of the guests? Where were my sisters and friends? Where were the flowers? I was told, "And don't worry, even though you are not having a big wedding you will have a wedding reception." What did it matter what I wanted anyway? I couldn't make it happen, so what the heck! Even though I didn't say anything to my future brother-in-law, somehow he knew how I was feeling and what I was thinking. He said to me, "If you don't want to get married, then don't!" I looked at him because I really didn't want to get married in Las Vegas in a chapel and I wasn't sure if I wanted to marry Michael. At that point, I felt I didn't have enough time to think. Was I doing the right thing? After all, the Bible does say not to be unequally yoked. (2 Corinthians 6:14) I asked myself, "Am I making a huge mistake? I am only seventeen!"

We were definitely unequally yoked. I was a Christian who was backsliding fast. I was actually going against a lot of the things I had been taught. Michael didn't go to church and he didn't want me to go sometimes. The church meant the world to me, even though the older I got, the further I drifted away from the things I knew were right. Michael was a drinker and a smoker and I wasn't. Spiritually we were not compatible, but for some reason I loved him. He was funny and we had so much fun together. I knew that I wasn't doing the right thing, but we were having a baby and it seemed only right to get married and take care of this baby together.

Having a baby is one thing and making more mistakes is another. We were young and we were ignoring all the warning signs. Even though we talked many nights about getting married, it just didn't seem like this was the right time. Why didn't I just say no.? Why didn't I stop the wedding? Why didn't he stop the wedding? His father wasn't even there. No one from his family was there to witness our day of matrimony, not even his mother. It all just seemed so wrong!

I Now Pronounce You Man and Wife

Standing at the alter scared to death, I said, "I do." The minister said, "I now pronounce you man and wife, you may now kiss the bride." We kissed and looked at everyone or shall I say the few people that were there. They all looked so happy for us. I don't know what I was feeling. I smiled, but I don't know why I smiled because I was numb.

Of course we went out on the town. Michael gambled and I shopped. It was fun being out and together. It was fun until that night when it was time to go to the hotel. I guess you could call it our honeymoon suite. Wishful thinking I guess! I remember it wasn't what I imagined the honeymoon suite to be. It was just a little old hotel room. I didn't like it at all but I didn't say anything. I was trying to fake it but I couldn't. No matter how hard I tried I couldn't. I wanted to scream and run away somewhere. My "HUSBAND" was trying to get with his wife on their wedding night and be romantic, but I wasn't mentally prepared to do that. I just couldn't make myself do it. No matter how hard I tried, I couldn't. The pain of it all was almost unbearable. I just couldn't make love to him! I felt so bad for him, but emotionally I was a wreck. I didn't want him to feel bad but I just wasn't able. My body wouldn't respond. I didn't want him to touch me at all. Finally he got the message and he rolled over and went to sleep. I silently felt my warm tears as they rolled down my face on the pillow as I cried myself to sleep! Thank God for sleep. I didn't know how much more I could have taken. Mentally I was unstable!

Thank God for the morning. I felt a little better and my wonderful, very understanding husband was still there. We got up, dressed, and met everyone else for breakfast. My husband and I had some money to spend but we couldn't come to an agreement on the second day of our marriage. He wanted to gamble and I wanted to shop. We divided the money and he gambled and I shopped until we both were broke.

Well, when all of our money is gone, it was time to go home. It was a nice drive home. My dad and my husband did a lot of talking in the back seat. When we made it back to L.A., I went into my mother's house to gather my things. I was piddling around the house while my husband was patiently waiting to take me to our new home. I really didn't want to leave my childhood home.

I can recall many nights my mother would tell me not to stay over to Michael's house all night and I would fall asleep and stay anyway. Now that I was entitled to go and stay all night, I didn't want to. Why do we always want to do what we are not supposed to do? And what we are suppose to do we don't want to do! My mother noticed my hesitation and she said, "Girl you better go, your husband is out there waiting for you." I said, "Mommy, I don't want to go, can't I stay here for the night?" She said, "No, you are married now and you have to go home with your husband." I just looked at her and walked slowly to the door and down the steps and got into the car. Looking back as we pulled off, I could have cried. "I am too young to be doing this," I remember thinking to myself, "And, I'm about to have a baby!"

Cohabitation wasn't easy for either of us, but we were trying to make it work. I imagined things were especially difficult for him because not only were we newlyweds, but we were about to be parents. Anybody knows a pregnant woman is hard to please. I remember being hungry in the middle of the night and I would wake Michael up and ask him to fix me a peanut butter and jelly sandwich. He didn't fix it any kind of way. He would put the peanut butter on one slice of bread and placed it in the oven to let it get warm, and then he would take it out and put the other slice of bread with strawberry jelly on it on top. Umm good! That was my favorite sandwich and nobody could fix it for me like him. He tried very hard to deal with a pregnant wife and her needs. In the beginning, it was fun playing house, but pregnancy was getting difficult for me.

Attending school was becoming stressful because I had to walk up and down two flights of stairs and walk from one end of campus to the other. It was no longer fun because they took away my sports when they found out I was eight months pregnant and playing badminton. I couldn't drive and was forced to catch the city bus. It just seemed logical to drop out of school and go back a few months after the baby was born.

We had some problems with our neighbors. They broke into our house and stole some things. We couldn't believe our friends would do this to us and I was afraid to continue to stay there. There would be times when my husband wasn't home at night and I would be home alone and I didn't like that. I conveniently worked it out so my mother's tenant would move out of the back house (the house my sister used to live in) into our current place and we would move into the "back house." The only thing wrong with these arrangements were that when the manager of our old place found out, he didn't want my friend to live there even though she was paying rent. She had to find another place to stay. I was so sorry but I wasn't going to give up my mother's place. It was subconsciously my way of getting back home where I felt safe. I know it was wrong, but I did it anyway. We made sure that my friend found another place to stay. Now I was somewhat back at home doing fine, so I thought.

We really were not ready for marriage. We had no clue of how to commit to one another or how to deny ourselves, one for the other. We were so young, and with no marriage counseling we were doomed to fail. I guess we felt because we loved each other and enjoyed being together all of the time, marriage would work for us. After all, getting married was the right thing for two people who loved each other and wanted to be together forever, so I thought. Once we got married, things began to change. It wasn't the same as when we were dating. We could hardly agree on anything anymore. For example, I wanted us to stay home together in the evenings, enjoy one another and plan our future together, and he wanted to come home after work and hang out with his friends and brothers drinking and having fun. I guess I could have run the streets too, but I didn't think that was what a newly married couple should be doing. Sometimes our friends would come to our house and drink and play dominos and that made it a little better.

As long as he was home we were not arguing or fighting. I know a man needs his space, but I also know if you are in the streets all of the time, something wrong is bound to happen. As a married couple we began to butt heads.

Michael was smoking cigarettes, and was constantly telling me he needed to quit. One day in particular, we didn't have much money and he wanted to take our last few dollars and buy some cigarettes. In attempts to save our money and help him quit I locked the door and took the key. He got so mad, he climbed out the window and left. I can also recall one night when we fought about something and somehow I ended up on the floor. I was nine months pregnant and he was kicking me in my back. I don't know if he was trying to kick my stomach, but I was trying hard to cover my belly, so I laid there in a fetal position in an attempt to protect my baby. When I got up, I called out the window to my mother for help. Mamma came to the back house and asked, "What is wrong with you?" He told her, "I'm leaving and I want my ring back!" Momma replied, "If you want to leave you can go, but you are not going to get that ring back!" The nerve of him doing such a thing! He got mad and left. I was so upset I called his dad and brothers to see if they would talk to him, but I was told I needed to work it out myself. They didn't want to get involved.

I was only eighteen years old and I didn't know what to do. What has happened to the man I knew for the past four years? We had only been married for about six months and our world seemed to be falling apart. I didn't know that saying; "I do" would make such a difference in a relationship. Maybe he was feeling trapped or he didn't really want to be married. I didn't really know what the problem was. He was a good man at times and would flip out at times. My mother tried to help us as much as she could. My husband always worked despite constantly switching jobs. This was something I wasn't used to because my father worked the same job until he retired. I was used to a man providing for his family. Even though my father drank and got on my mother's nerves at times, he never failed to go to work, and he always gave my mother the check. He never hit my mother, Never! To be going through what I was going through was foreign to me. If he didn't want to be here, why did he marry me? Deep down inside I would say to myself,

"I knew it, I knew it, I knew it."

It's Time

Amid the fussing, fighting and making up it was finally time for our baby to arrive. My mother had me preparing all week because she had a feeling the baby was coming soon. My husband and I attended the Lamas classes and my bags were packed. While in the shower, the pains hit. I stayed in the shower for a long time because I was afraid to get out and tell my mom that I was having contractions. I was thinking to myself, "How can I get out of this? How can I have this baby another way?" As I was letting the water run down my back and thinking intensely how to turn this whole situation around, the pains were intensifying.

The water began to get cold so I had to get out. I got dressed and went into the dining room and sat quietly at the table. I decided not to tell anyone that I was having contractions. I sat there until I couldn't take it anymore. I got up and started walking around the table. Around and around I went. The same table

I ran around when my mother found out I was pregnant the first time. Finally my mother came into the dining room and she asked, "What are you doing?" I told her, "I am having contractions!" She said, "Get a watch so we can time them." By then they were close. She told me to call my husband and have him put the bags in the car. My mother had encouraged me to call the doctor several times but I wouldn't. I told her I was going to wait a little while longer. It wasn't that I felt I should wait any longer; I was trying to stall for time. I needed more time "before delivering the baby. I was scared to death. I was afraid of the pain. I wanted to have the baby but I didn't want to give birth. I know it sounds crazy but I wanted another way out. Finally, my mother insisted that I call the doctor. When I called him and told him how close the contractions were, he started yelling and said, "You need to get to the hospital right away!"

My husband was driving, my mom was in the front seat and I was sliding all over the back seat as he raced to the hospital. When I got there they put us in a room and my husband made sure he had my bags. We had a rolling pin, tennis balls and all kinds of stuff. I needed to dilate just a little bit more. My husband, bless his heart, was only trying to do what we had learned in the class. During that time it seemed like so much fun. It was so romantic working together to bring forth this baby, but when the real moment had arrived, I didn't want him to touch me!

When he took the tennis balls out of the bag and started to roll them on my back I yelled, "DON'T TOUCH ME!" I didn't want to see a tennis ball. The pain was intense! It was unbearable! I didn't think that I was going to be able to deliver this baby.

Fortunately for me, after what seemed to be a lifetime of waiting, I finally gave birth to a healthy eight pound, fourteen ounce baby boy. My husband says to this day, that all men need to see their children being born, because it will make a difference. As soon as he came out of the womb I told my husband, "Check his fingers and toes!" Michael said, "I checked them baby and they are all there." I always wanted to have a boy first, then a girl, so my little girl would have a big brother. That's something I never had. God gave me what I wanted.

The recovery was wonderful. I had a private room at Cedars Sinai Hospital in Beverly Hills. It was lovely! My mother had given me this beautiful baby pink gown with a matching robe and I remember walking down the hall, so peaceful and so happy I had given birth to a healthy baby boy. We named the baby after his father. Michael was so proud! I must admit when the baby was first born, he wouldn't take his eyes off of his dad. I was trying to get him to look at me so I could see his eyes but for some reason he just stared at his dad. It was such a wonderful sight to behold, a proud father gazing in the eyes of his son. All of this was bitter sweet because three days later I checked out of the hospital and I had to leave my baby behind because he had jaundice. I was able to go visit with him everyday.

May 8th was a gloomy, rainy Mother's Day when the hospital called and told me that I could come and pick up my baby. I was so happy. I screamed and jumped for joy. When we arrived back to my mother's house we carefully walked up the wet steps of the front porch. My mother greeted us at the front door with the biggest smile on her face. As she walked out onto the porch, she stretched forth her arm catching raindrops. With a few raindrops on her fingertips, she placed them on the baby's forehead and blessed her first grandchild. It was a beautiful moment in time! My husband fell in love with his son from day one. I knew then that they would be inseparable. I thought maybe now we can be one big happy family.

We had our good days and we still had our bad days. He wanted to hang out with his friends. I couldn't run the streets because I had to, or shall I say, I wanted to stay home with our son. I had no problem staying home because I wasn't accustomed to going out and being in the streets. I would be sad but I would also try to understand. It seemed the more understanding I tried to be; the more he took advantage of it.

Eventually I said to myself, "If you can't beat 'em join 'em." I started drinking and smoking marijuana. Now we were on one accord and most of the time the gatherings were at our house on the weekend. Party over here! In attempts to make things work, our family issues were getting worse for me. At the time it was subtle and I didn't recognize what was going on but I knew it wasn't right. I remember when my husband would be gone to work and I would be home alone with the baby, I wanted to get high. One time in particular when we didn't have any weed, I decided to hit a cigarette butt. I was new at smoking cigarettes and it gave me a buzz and I felt like I was high off marijuana. My husband told me I should stop doing that or else I was going to get hooked on both. I totally disagreed, and I felt I could handle it and stay in control. I did manage, but only for a while. I knew this wasn't healthy, yet I did it anyway. And we call ourselves being a family!

Chapter 4 Wilding Out!

One day the father of a friend came to my door. He said, “Tell your husband he better stay away from my daughter or else I’m going to kill him!” I asked, “What are you talking about?” He told me,“ Just tell your husband what I said and he will know what you’re talking about!” I wondered what in the world was going on! All day I had time to think and my mind started to put things together. My husband was a cab driver and at times his checks were short. He always gave me some crazy excuse as to why this was. Later on, the girl’s brother came over and I asked him, “What is going on with your sister?” He told me, “Your husband and my sister have been riding out by the beach during the day when he was supposed to be working.” Well, I knew how much my husband liked the beach because that is where we courted all the time. I couldn’t wait for him to come home and ask him what was going on.

I didn't know if any of this was true, so I was trying to figure out how to handle the situation. Once he got home, I let him get settled. After being there a while, I told him what the girl's father said. He told me nothing was going on. He did confess to riding her to the beach but he said that they never did anything. Of course, I didn't believe him and I wanted him to fess up. I gave him an ultimatum. I told him, "If you are messing with that girl, I want you to get your things and leave." He got up and took some of his stuff and left. He maintained his innocence after that night. Often I would ask him if he really was innocent, why did he leave? He claims I put him out, but if he really didn't want to leave, he should have fought for his innocence. He didn't say anything to defend himself; he just got up and left as if he didn't want to be there anyway.

The way I figured it, if he really didn't want to be there then he shouldn't stay. I didn't want anyone to be with me if they didn't want to. I must admit I was floored when he left. I couldn't believe my husband had just walked out on me. The same man I gave up my virginity to, married, and had his baby. I felt everything I had turned my back on God to get was for NOTHING! I should have kept on being a good girl. I should have stayed in church and kept doing the right thing. Now I am going to be a divorcee with a child.

I decided to forget about my husband and make a life for my son and me. I was going to pick myself up and make it without him. I didn't need Michael in my life and I was going to show him just that. I did think from time to time that he would come back home but he didn't. He would always come by and see our son, then he would leave.

The more he visited my son, the madder I got. I thought, "Once again I try to do something right and it all goes wrong." I thought that getting married would mean something. He didn't want to come home and he said that he wanted a divorce but he wasn't going to pay for it and I was certainly not going to pay, so we just separated. Why did we get married in the first place? I would have rather had the baby out of wedlock than to end up divorced. I felt since he left the house he should pay for the divorce. I wasn't going to worry myself with the details. Just bring me the papers and if I agreed, I would sign them. In the meantime, I was going to do my thing regardless of if I was married or not. I said, "Forget it, I am going to go all out and I am going to enjoy life."

My real intentions were to make Michael jealous. I wanted him to be sorry that he ever left me. It was a very painful time for me. I would sometimes think we should have just remained boyfriend and girlfriend. Maybe we were just too young to be married. Maybe the pressure of the baby was too much. I hated going through all of this. I gained a baby but I lost a husband/friend in the process. One thing I knew for sure, I was too proud to beg! I guess you could say it was pride, but when I really think about it, begging someone to stay with you is just something you don't do. If they want to go, then let them go. My father would always tell me, "If some one doesn't want to play with you then don't beg them to stay and play, let them go home. Find some one else to play with you and someone who likes playing the things you like to play." Why should I beg him to stay with me if he wasn't going to be happy? Go make yourself happy! I will get over it. Besides, I was accustomed to pain!

I was all too familiar with being hurt by people. I figured if I had survived before I would again. After all, I was good at suppressing my pain and going on as if everything was fine. I would actually believe that I was okay when in reality I was just ignoring the symptoms. I got myself together and found a job at a bank making good money. I bought myself another car, and I was fine all by myself taking care of my baby boy. He was my pride and joy. With the help of my family and friends we survived. His daddy remained a part of his life and mine too. He would be nice and cordial when he saw me but that was as far as it went. I started to go out and party at the clubs with my sister and friends, which was something that I had never done before.

At the time I decided to start going out to the clubs, I was a size eighteen. Most of the night I would just sit there and have a few drinks. I didn't get asked to dance very much. That was okay, even though I really wanted to dance and I wanted to be attractive to the men like the other ladies were. I dealt with it and I made the best of the time while I was there. For a long time while I was married a lot of my friends were going out but I wouldn't not go. I felt there was nothing out there for me. When my husband left me I said forget it, just go out and see what it is all about. I soon realized that I wasn't missing anything but since I was single, I figured it was better than sitting home alone every weekend.

When my husband found out I was going to the club he told me he didn't like it but what could he do about it? Nothing! He didn't want me, so why did he care about what I was doing? I don't know why I didn't start going back to church. Just go back to what I knew was right. Why would I put myself out there on the chopping block? I had heard about the clubs growing up and I knew it was no place for a nice young lady. I knew there was trouble at the clubs. Trouble always found me. I remember learning in church the club was the enemy's territory and anything was subject to go down. I knew it wasn't the place I should be but at this point in my life I really didn't care anymore. I was going to work, take care of my responsibilities and have fun!

While I was working I was also being very productive. I started to save money and put new furniture on lay-a-way. I engulfed myself in work. I became obsessed with working and making money. If I was asked to work overtime I had no problem with it. I didn't have to worry about a baby sitter because my mother and sisters would gladly watch my baby. He was the first grandchild and he was a boy. He was well taken care of. I think working was part of my way of not dealing with my feelings. My supervisors loved me because I worked hard and I would work as long as they wanted me to. I would even work on the weekend if they needed me.

If it was the weekend and I had to work late, on my way home I stopped by the liquor store and picked up strawberry margaritas and beef jerky. I would go home alone, take a bath, put on some good music, have a drink, smoke (marijuana) and crash. I would party at home by myself. It didn't matter to me because I was content with doing my thing. I wasn't bothering anybody and I didn't want anyone bothering me. I figured everyone would be better off that way. My shift began at two in the evening or sometimes noon. I had the mornings to spend with my child. On the weekends I spent most of the day with him. His dad was still coming by to see him. They would always have a good time together.

My son meant the world to me. I thought he was the most beautiful child in the world. One day when he was about seven months old he messed in his diaper really bad and I needed a towel to clean him up. He was in the mood to play and I couldn't get him to keep still. I didn't want to pick him up and take him to the bathroom because I needed my hands free to get a soapy, wet towel. After several attempts I looked at him and I said with authority and my finger in the air, "You lay there and don't you move!" His legs slammed down on the bed and he rested there perfectly still looking at me as if to say, "Okay!" I hurried into the bathroom and got the wet towel and ran back to the bed only to find him in the same position I left him. He didn't move until I said something to him and then he started playing around again. While I was cleaning him I said to myself, "I know this is going to be a very obedient child" and for the most part that is how he has been all of his life. There were very few times I had to spank him. Most of the time all I had to do was talk to him and he would listen and obey. I admired that about him.

At work I kept seeing this guy who looked familiar to me. One day we had the pleasure of meeting and to my surprise, he was my best friend from elementary school. Right away we hooked up again. We started spending time together because we had the same work schedule. On the weekends we would hang out at my house. Most of the time he would fall asleep and I would take him home in the morning. I remember one morning my mother saw me taking him home and she asked me who he was and I told her he was just a good friend that I worked with. She told me, "That does not look good, having men leaving your house early in the morning." I told her, "We weren't doing anything except listening to music, having a few drinks and we fell asleep." That was the honest truth. She was trying to tell me to be concerned with what the neighbors were thinking. I knew we weren't doing anything wrong.

I felt the neighbors could think whatever they wanted. I didn't care! They were going to think the worst anyway. Besides, I was getting tired of people pleasing and getting nothing but hurt in return. At this point in my life I was going to do what I wanted to do and how I wanted to do it and I didn't care what anyone thought about it! I was tired of hurting, tired of trying to people please, and tired of people hurting me and treating me any way they wanted. I used to be a quiet little girl but I felt myself coming out. It was on now! One thing about me though, I didn't set out to hurt anyone. I always minded my own business and I did my own thing. What ever I wanted, I got. I wasn't going to depend on anyone and if you tried to get in my business I would let you know how I felt about it. I just wanted to be left alone.

We Were Taught To Be Independent

As young girls growing up I remember my father teaching us to be independent, yet knowing whom to depend on. I remember when my father owned some apartments and we would have go with him after a tenant had moved out to help him prepare the apartment for the next renter. We learned how to replace glass panes, screens, paint, unstop pipes, and numerous other tasks. We even had to mow the lawn with a push lawn mower. One day I went out to my car and I had a flat tire. I rushed back into the house to tell my dad I needed my tire changed. He came outside right away. He walked over to the car and stood there and I stood there also. He was waiting on me and I was waiting on him. After standing there for a short period I asked him what was he waiting on? He told me, "I am not going to change the tire but I will show you how to do it." He was trying to teach me to do one more thing I might need to know how to do one day. I learned that day how to change my own tire and believe it or not I did have to use that knowledge not too long afterwards.

At this point and time in my life I felt knowing how to be an independent woman was a great asset for me because I was finding it very hard to depend on anyone! My daddy wanted us to know how to work well with others, but if we had to do it alone, he wanted us to know how to take care of ourselves. I had no problem doing that!

So my gentlemen friend and I became a team. I would tell people he was my brother. When we went out to a club if he wanted to dance with other ladies he did and if I wanted to dance with other guys I did. We really were only just friends. I really did like having guys as good friends. It seemed it was less friction to have a guy as a friend than it was to have a female. Don't get me wrong, I had some wonderful girlfriends and I still do but I also had a lot of male friends that I really enjoyed being with. One day at our job this young guy came to work for our company and for some reason we befriended him and we did a lot of socializing after work together. He was still staying with his parents so he wasn't at liberty to stay out all night like we were.

On Friday nights we usually worked long hours and it was too late to go to the club when we got off. We would get some drinks and go to my place and chill. The very first time we all got together at my house we fell asleep on the floor. When we woke up it was dawn and he had been out all night. I had to hurry and take him home, hoping he didn't get into too much trouble. Of course I had to hear about it from my mother again. I didn't care what people had to say because I knew we were three innocent people just hanging out and having fun and there was no sex involved. For some reason people seem to think it is impossible for two people of the opposite gender to be together and not be sexually active. I had a lot of male friends with whom I wasn't sexually active. Like I mentioned before, I had gotten to the point where I didn't care what people thought of me. At least that's what I told myself.

By continuing to go the clubs, dancing every now and then, smoking pot and hardly eating because I was working so hard, I had lost a lot of weight. I was no longer a size eighteen. I had really slimmed down. To my amazement the slimmer I got, the more attention I received and all of that attention wasn't good for me!

Weekends With My Son

On the weekends my son and I would dress alike and go out on the town in Los Angeles where there is always something going on and somewhere to go. I would get up, clean my house and car, get dressed and off we went. I can remember having a lot of fun at this point and time in my life. When my son was about two years old his paternal grandparents would often pick him up and take him shopping at Sears. He always enjoyed going with them. Even though his dad and I were not living together, we were still married and he was being well taken care of. My husband and my mother were becoming closer and closer. They were getting so close I believe that I was beginning to get jealous. My mother would watch my son and Michael would have to deal with her as far as my son was concerned.

My husband had fallen on bad times and my mother would have him do little things around the business to help put some money in his pocket. Sometimes I just wanted him to go away. My mother would tell me to leave him alone, let him spend the night if he needed a place to stay. She really did like my baby's daddy. He was doing odd jobs here and there. He couldn't let his son know when he was down on his luck. He often picked my son up and took him to the park or to the beach. Michael didn't have any problem spending time with his son. I didn't have a problem with it but sometimes I just didn't want to be bothered with him at all.

Do the Hustle

I began to meet a lot of guys who were hustlers. There was nothing I wanted that someone wasn't selling or knew someone who was selling it. I was being introduced to a world I had only seen in the movies or heard about on the news. I was warned about this kind of life in the church, but I never in a million years thought I would become part of it.

I decided to get in on the action. Everyone I was beginning to meet had some kind of hustle. Making money was nothing new to me because as a child, when I was in elementary school my dad taught us how to take a dollar and make two or three dollars. I recall one day when the ice cream truck was coming down the street, my sisters and I ran in the house and was screaming for some ice cream. My dad heard us, and he told us, "No!" Of course we whined because we wanted some ice cream. My dad took us to the store and bought us a box of ice cream and told us we could eat some of the ice cream, sell some and take the money we made and go and buy another box. Sometimes that is what we did and sometimes we sneaked and bought ice cream off the truck anyway. But I loved the concept.

As a young child I loved to turn a dollar (make a profit). I recall in the fourth or fifth grade, when I was playing the flute, I would go to the little corner store and buy penny candy and put it in my flute case. I would come home and sell it to the kids in the neighbor hood for a nickel. These were kids who were not allowed to go to the store so they were my customers. I made a lot of money doing that and I really liked seeing the money grow.

On my job there was a lady who sold clothes and I would purchase numerous items from her. I was always amazed at the size I could fit. I was still not used to the weight I had lost. She sold designer clothes I couldn't afford to buy in the store. Okay I will say it; I was buying hot clothes on the job. No one seemed to mind. During my break I would try them on and make a deal. My cousin Shelly had a friend who used to sell hot clothes and I started buying from her also. I was sharp all of the time. One day on my job one of my co-workers gave me the nickname, "Chic". I was known as Sha Chic. I even had a personalized licensed plate made for my car that read, "Sha Chic." When my husband and I were still together I stole a dress from JC Penney and I had to go to jail. I was utterly humiliated and embarrassed and I knew stealing wasn't for me and I never stole from a department store again. I decided to leave stealing to the professionals. I would find a hustle and make more money to buy from the pros that stole and stole well, and I knew a lot of them.

Speaking of a nickel, it reminds me of the time I was molested by the old man around the corner. I had already been molested before when I was about ten years old. It happened several times and then it just stopped. I know for a fact that as a child I didn't deal with this type of abuse properly and I am sure it played a part in my demise. All I know is I was happy it stopped. He was the second person to molest me and after he did it he would give me a nickel to go to the store. Why I didn't go to my parents, I don't know. As a child, when this sort of thing happens to you and you know it's wrong, even though it is not your fault for initiating it, you feel for some unknown reason it is. You feel too ashamed to tell someone because of what might be said about you even though it's not your fault. I will save this story for later.

When I was younger my neighbor taught me arts and crafts and I capitalized on it. I was able to make shawls, and baby's blankets and sell them. The neighborhood children and me would put on concerts and sell food and make money. The only difference between then and now, I wasn't used to making illegal money. I was starting to dibble and dabble into an area I knew I shouldn't. I was out there and I was feeling that I was invincible. So now I had to get me a hustle.

Since I was smoking weed, I decided to cut out the middleman. I purchased a half of a pound of marijuana, sold some and I smoked the rest for free.

That's what I did. I sold to my friends, neighbors and even to my supervisor. Yes, that's what I said, my supervisor. I tell you, the more is exposed to you the more your mouth falls open in disbelief. I was a roller now. I had a job, a hustle, and I always had a bankroll.

I remember sometimes when I would come home from work I would come through my mom's house before going to the "back house" where I lived and I would give her a wad of money. She would ask me where I got the money from and I told her that it was my money. After all she was taking care of my son. It was only right to kick her down (give her some). My mother would warn me I better not be doing anything wrong and I better stop running around with different types of people because I would find myself in a trick bag. Well, I wasn't even hearing it. Sha Chic was rolling and handling her business. I knew people and I was constantly meeting more underground people all of the time. I was even introduced to the people with the cocaine. That was not my bag. I wasn't going to be snorting that stuff up my nose. I had my limits on getting high, but I must say I was moving faster and faster everyday and I didn't realize how fast I was moving. People would give me powdered cocaine wrapped up in white paper. I had heard you were supposed to keep it in the freezer, so when they gave it to me I acted like I appreciated it, but I would take it home and put it in the freezer. I wasn't interested in trying it.

Chapter 5
Demons in the Club

The first time I went to the Carolina West on Century Boulevard in Los Angeles, I had a ball. I have always loved music and they played my favorite tunes. It was loud and I just loved it. I danced all night long. When we left the club I couldn't wait until we were going to go again. I must have planted a dangerous seed that night. Whenever anyone wanted to go I was ready. There were days when I wanted to go and my friends wouldn't have the money so I would pay their way. When I was ready to party I was ready to party. It had gotten so bad, when I went to the club and heard a song I liked and no one came over and asked me to dance, I would get out on the dance floor and dance by myself. I didn't care what people thought of me. I had paid my money to get in and I came to have a good time and I did. Whatever it took, I had a good time. Sometimes my sister and I would dance together. Most of the time if I did get up and start dancing by myself someone would come and ask me to dance. Once I had a few drinks in me, I didn't care. I partied! Yes, I had started drinking!

Courvoisier with limejuice was my favorite drink. There was a certain type of limejuice I could only get from "Johnny's liquor" on Adams Boulevard. I would have the juice in my purse and would order Courvoisier and pour it in. Sometimes I would have a Rum and Coke. After that it was live, live, "slippity slide". (An old saying we said when we partied). The party was on. I didn't realize how much I liked to dance until I started going out to the clubs. I wasn't sure what everyone else was there for but I knew I was there for one reason and one reason only and that was to get on the dance floor, dance and have a good time. I wasn't looking for anything else but to have a good time. Not a man or anything. After all I was still married but separated. I just wanted to party.

It seemed the more I went, the more I wanted to go. It had become my favorite past time. I didn't have a problem talking one of my girlfriends into going. Most of the time my sister, Santa and I would go together. If we went on Thursday I would have to get up in the morning and go to work and she would have to get go to school. It didn't matter how early in the morning we came home, we were able to get up and handle our business. Young blood I guess.

The amazing thing about it was we were still living at our parent's house (I was back and forth from the back house to the front house).

I guess as long as we got up and were responsible my parents were okay with it. For now that is!

What started out as fun ultimately turned out to not be good for me at all. It wasn't until I started smoking marijuana that I realized it was so many different kinds. Some marijuana was a lot more potent than others, which meant you got a lot higher. I have experienced smoking regular marijuana, Panama Red, Columbian Gold, PCP, and angel dust. Not everybody was privileged to the really good stuff. In order for me to come in contact with these various levels of drugs I was introduced to some very interesting people. I was always meeting someone new. For some reason, people wanted to turn me on to the new stuff. I would really get high. One thing I found out quick and that was PCP and angel dust was too much for me. I couldn't stand that high. It made me feel really weird.

I Meet Mr. "D" at the Club

One night some friends and I were at the club and I met this guy. He was kind of cool and he was cute I thought. He was very bow legged, heavy set, and he had a Jheri Curl. As he was approaching our table we were wondering who he was going to ask to dance. I really didn't think he was going to ask me to dance but he did. We danced together several times that night. I believe we even slowed danced. I really did like him. I mean I really liked him. I believe I would have liked anyone who showed any interest in me. At the end of the night he asked me for my phone number and I gave it to him. I thought about him all night. I could hardly wait for him to give me a call.

By the time I met “D” I had become very popular at the club. I knew a lot of people. I knew the bouncers, the bar tenders and a lot of regulars. I was a regular myself, and the life of the party. At least in our little corner anyway. We received VIP treatment and if there was an after party, we were invited. I really liked one of the bouncers I met but he considered me just a friend. I really wanted to be more than friends but he wasn’t having it. Not now anyway. Remember, what I wanted, I got! I knew it would be just a matter of time and I would have him. In the meantime I settled with just having him as a friend. He was really nice and he took care of us while we were there.

We partied Thursday through Saturday. It didn’t matter if we closed the place down on Sunday morning. It got so bad until my dad wanted to know what it was about this place that would make us act like that. What he didn’t understand was we just really liked to party. I would literally dance all night long. One night while my sister and I were out late, the bar tender said, “Last call for alcohol.” We were sitting at the table drinking our last drinks with about 20 people left in the club. I saw an older couple on the dance floor. They appeared to be a bit tipsy. I was sitting there focused on them, watching them have a good time and the more I looked I realized it was my father and his sister. I tapped my sister on the shoulder and told her to look and tell me I wasn't seeing what I thought I was seeing. As we both looked on in total disbelief, all of a sudden they fell on the floor. The DJ began to say something. All I know is we jumped up and took off running out of the club as fast as we could. We didn't want anyone to know we knew them and we didn't want them to see us. We left quickly without inquiring to see how they were going to get home or if they were ok. We just left.

Later that day we told our mom what happened. She told us, "He just had to go to the club and see what in the world was going on. He wanted to know what made his girls stay out all night long after he had asked them repeatedly not to do so." We just loved to dance and the Carolina West was the place to go if you wanted to party and get your dance on. We went to other clubs from time to time but my favorite was the "Carolina West".

Mr. "D" and I dated for a while. He was a dope dealer and he lived across town. He sold weed and made a lot of money doing it. He didn't have a regular job. It was strange too because he didn't have a car. He was always borrowing somebody's car. So we hooked up and became a pair. What I liked about him was he was really laid back and he loved to go out and have a good time. Even though he didn't have a car we were everywhere. If we were not at the club we were at a supper club. We would frequent "Concerts by the Sea." Whatever I wanted for the night I got, except him. There weren't too many nights that he would stay overnight but he would stay for a long time. But as you know, the longer you are around a person the more you find out.

Shortly into the relationship he started asking me to let him use my car while I was at work. At first I was hesitant but then I let him keep it. He would pick me up on time almost always. I can remember one day in particular he came to pick me up and he had a gentleman in the car with him. I just jumped in the back seat and I let him stay in the front. This way I could scope out things. While we were driving "D" asked me how was my day and we engaged in causal conversation. Then all of a sudden he hands me a "joint". He said, "Here hit this, it is hot off the boat." When I asked him what it was he said smiling, "Just try it and let me know how you like it." Then he and the guy just laughed. I began to hit the joint. I had a thirty-minute commute and by the time we arrived at my house I was pretty "lit" (high). I could barely get out of the car. "D" was laughing and asking me what was wrong. I could hardly walk. He so graciously helped me into the house and laid me across my bed. At that time I had a waterbed. Why did he put me on the bed? I felt like "Mr. Wizard" spinning in a funnel.

I could hear my mother yelling from her back door but I couldn't get up. "D" kept telling me she was calling me and I needed to get up but I couldn't. "D" became scared and he told my mother what was going on and they discussed possibly taking me to the hospital. If I had gone to the hospital I would have landed in jail. I was so high it took me until the next morning to come down. I was so mad at him. He told me I was weak and I couldn't handle the good stuff. He also said I really scared him though and he would never give me anymore. I told him, "Believe me I don't want anymore of that stuff." He had taken a joint (weed) and laced it with some cocaine that had been mixed with "Canebinol." It wasn't for me.

I was really beginning to like Mr." D". For his birthday I gave him a gold chain. He said he really liked it and every time I saw him he had it on. He loved to play basketball and would go away on the weekends. One day when he came over I noticed he didn't have the chain. He told me he was sorry, but he believed he lost it during one of his games. He told me with such sincerity, I believed him. Then again I didn't believe him!

Some time later he came by and he left his bag at my house while he went off somewhere. For some reason, I went through his bag and I found a letter from a girl. She was thanking him for giving her a gold necklace. When he returned to the house I confronted him and he gave me some lame excuse. I can't even remember what it was. We argued and he left. But, of course we got back together.

Things were beginning to get raggedy. I found out more and more about this wonderful mystery man. I decided to enjoy him and continue to put the pieces together. After all, I was still married and he wasn't talking about marrying me, but he said he loved me. Go figure! Well time was passing and I was getting older. As my 21st birthday approached, I decided to throw myself a big birthday bash at my mother's house. I asked her permission and she said yes. I was actually shocked. I knew a lot of people and I invited just about all of them. I had a live DJ, alcohol, weed and cocaine to snort.

I was about a size nine at this time and I wore a beautiful silver beaded dress. At first I was worried that no one was going to show because it was getting late, but then everyone arrived about the same time, except my man "D." It was okay though because I was celebrating me and I was going to have a good time with or without him. I truly did have a good time. I couldn't believe my parents were in their bedroom and they had fallen asleep. "D" didn't make it to my party but his best buddy was there. He was very handsome, slick and he was a dealer too. He drove a corvette, my dream car. After the party, my cousin and I were cleaning up and he stayed and helped. I was ready to go to sleep but he wouldn't leave. He wanted to stay the night with me and I told him I wasn't going to do anything with him. He wouldn't leave and I was exhausted. I slept on the couch with my birthday dress still on and he did too. I told him to get up and he said he just wanted to lie there and he wasn't going to do anything to me. So I let him. He did wrap his arms around me, but that was it.

He told me that "D" didn't deserve me. He said, "I have been trying to tell you all along that "D" was doing you wrong." He asked me, "Do you know where D is and why he couldn't be here tonight?" I told him, " 'D' said he had to go out of town to a basketball tournament." He said, "That's not true," and began to tell me the whole story. I was so tired I really didn't want to hear anything that he had to say. But the more he talked the more I knew I needed to listen.

He told me "D" had just had a baby by this girl and they had gone off to Las Vegas to get married. I was lying with my face towards the back of the couch and he was behind me. He couldn't see my face and I was glad. What he told me it broke my heart. He talked and went on and on as I fought back the tears. I believe I silently cried myself to sleep. The next thing I knew "D's" friend was waking me up to tell me he had to go. He told me he liked me all along and maybe he and I could hook up. I just smiled and let him out of the door. I took my clothes off and I got in my bed. It was still early and I was really tired from celebrating my 21st birthday.

Well when I finally did get up the next day, I thought about "D", the baby and the marriage. Why did he have to tell me this? I guess now was as good of a time as ever. I meditated on what I was going to tell him when I finally got the chance to see him. Or, was I ever going to see him again. He is a married man now. What a bummer. Later in the evening I finally heard from him and he was asking if he could come by. When he got there I was looking good in my beautiful gown and matching silk robe. I had some music playing softly and fixed me a drink.

Suddenly there was a knock at the door. It was "D". He walked in smiling like he always did, kissed me on the cheek and sat down on the couch. He began to ask me about the party and he told me his friend told him how nice it was. Really though, the people only came, got high and when everything was gone they left. He kept on trying to have casual conversation. Finally I said, "I hear there is a congratulations in order." He said, "What are you talking about (smiling at me)?" I sat there for a moment and when he didn't say anything. I just came right out and said; "Congratulations! I hear you are a married man now!" He looked like he turned two shades lighter. He didn't know what to say to me. His smile left his face. I kept sipping my drink and waiting for a response. He began to explain why he got married. He told me the marriage really didn't mean anything it was just something that he had to do. He said, "Why do you think I'm over here with you and not home with her?" I told him, "I don't know, but because you are a married man you really need to go home and be with your wife." He really wanted to stay but I wouldn't let him. I wouldn't do anything with him except let him out the front door. He was highly upset and so was I, but I didn't let it show. I opened the front door and after standing there a while he finally walked out. I closed the door, turned the music up, sat on the couch, drank and cried. I also had a long talk with myself.

I made up in my mind I was no longer going to be used by the guys I met. I knew now that it was all a game. Most of the guys I was meeting were out in the street just to have fun and get what they could get. They were willing to say and do what ever it took to make it happen. It was a game I needed to hurry up and learn how to play if I was going to be out here.

Why would I let myself think someone was going to be with me when I was still married? Sex and drugs, drugs and sex, that is all it was about and a whole lot of people fooling themselves and being fooled. "I have had enough and I am going to play the game just like they are playing!" I said. From now on, what does love have to do with it?

The sad thing is I knew this was no way for a lady to live her life, but I was out there and I was really hurting. When I sat and thought about all of the good times, the lies, the deception and how big of a fool I allowed someone to make of me, I became even more angry, bitter, and cold. We'll if nothing else I was going to miss all of the fun Mr. D and I used to have together. Oh well, I am on my own again.

Even though Mr. D and I were no longer a pair he would still feel at liberty to stop by from time to time. One day I had some people come by the house to talk about doing business with me. I was letting them sample some of what I had to offer. I guess it was so good they stayed too long and all of a sudden there was a knock at my front door. They immediately said it must be their friend who they left in the car. I opened the door and there stood this tall, lean, dark, handsome black man.

For the first few moments we just stared at each other. I was speechless; he was so fine to me. I asked him to come in and he smiled at me with his beautiful white teeth. He came in, had a seat and we finished talking business. As everyone was leaving, we talked briefly. I was hoping he would ask for my phone number and he did. When he stepped out the door and began to walk away, he kept looking back at me not saying a word. I said to myself, "Well, as quick as one leaves another one comes." It wasn't long before (lets call him Peter) Peter called me and we began seeing each other.

One night Peter called and he wanted to come by and watch the fight. I told him it would be okay.

When he arrived, the fight hadn't started yet and my son was at the house. He was watching something on television. I had planned to take him to my mom's house when the fight started so Peter and I could be alone. Peter wanted me to turn the channel. I wasn't going to do that. I mean come on. I felt he had just arrived on the scene and already he wanted me to put him before my son. He got mad and told me that if I didn't turn the channel he was going to leave. I immediately got up and opened the front door and let him out of my house. He thought I was going to change my mind, but I didn't. The rules have changed now; I am not the same old girl anymore. I could see already this wasn't going to work.

Another time Peter called and wanted to come over and I told him he could. He came by and we were watching television and then there was a knock at the door. To my surprise it was "D". I let him in and told him he could have a seat. As we were all sitting there, I asked myself, "Oh shoot, what do I do now?" Then "D" got up and went into the kitchen and asked me to come in there with him. He asked me, "What's up?" I said, "What do you mean what's up?" He asked me, "Who is that Negro?" I told him, "Peter, my friend Peter." I walked back in the living room and sat down. Mr. D got himself something to drink and came back in the living room and said, "It's getting crowded in here!" My friend Peter looked at me and I said, "I know it's getting crowded so I think you need to leave." I went to the door and I opened it to let D out. Well "D" couldn't believe I did that to him. He's a married man and had the balls to think he was going to come to my house and still have the same status. NOT!

A few minutes after I let him out of the house there was another knock at the door and when I opened it, it was "D" again. He wanted me to come outside so we could talk. I told Peter I would be right back. We walked to the end of the driveway and sat on the bumper of one of the cars and began to talk. "D" really didn't want our relationship to end but what was I supposed to do? Be the other woman and put up with all of the drama that it brings? I knew I was still married also, but my husband and I had nothing to do with each another. I wasn't going to knowingly have a relationship with a married man and subject his wife to that kind of betrayal. Mr. "D" had lied to me for so long, but because we had so much fun together, I just ignored it. I would always say, as long as he treats me right, when he comes around it's okay with me.

Because he got married and lied to me about it, I knew it was time to let him go. As much as I hated to, I had to let him go. I felt like I had been played like a cheap deck of cards. Then again maybe not! I know he really cared for me but I also knew he had been put in a position and he had to make a choice. Because he chose her, I knew he had to let me go. I wasn't going to be his play toy. Besides, if he chose to make a commitment he needed to be faithful to her. Nothing he said that night could make me change my mind. If I had not found someone else so quickly I might have reconsidered, then again I don't know. He cried and begged me not to do this, but I knew it was the right thing to do. It would only be a matter of time before his wife would find out about me. It wasn't right and I didn't want to have that type of relationship. Now that I know she actually exists, I have to say goodbye. It wasn't an easy decision to make because I really do believe I fell in love with him.

He left and I went back into the house. As soon as I sat down Peter asked me, "Who was that and what's going on?" Before I could explain he said, "You know, I think I'm just going to leave!" He got up and headed for the door. I didn't even put up a fight or plea. I said okay and walked him to the door. He left and didn't look back (like he used to always do). I closed the door and sat back down on the couch. I said with a giggle, "One minute you have a house full, the next minute you have nobody!" Oh well!

After a few days Peter gave me a call and said he wanted to stop by and bring his friend for just a minute. I said, "Okay come on." When they arrived they headed straight for the kitchen and asked me, "Are you expecting anyone?" I told him, "No." He was really rushing like he was in a big hurry. I was wondering what was going on. He said, "Can you get me a spoon?" I gave him one. Then he said, "Do you have a belt?" I got him a belt wondering all the while, "What does he need all of this stuff for?" The two of them sat there and started preparing heroine to shoot up. I left the kitchen and closed the door and sat down. Then I heard, "Sha" I said, "Yes," he said, "Come here!" So I went back into the kitchen and he asked me to hold the belt while he shot up. He told me to hold it really tight. So I did. When he put the needle in and pulled it back out, I saw blood coming out. I let go of the belt and ran out of the kitchen. He started yelling at me. I was so scared! I was furious! I was mad! I was mad at him for doing that stuff in my house. I know I did a lot of things that weren't right, but that is one thing I didn't like playing around with.

He finished and balled me out. I told him I was sorry but he really scared me. I didn't tell him what I really wanted to tell him but I vowed to myself I would never let that happen again. It wasn't going to work for Peter and me. This was the final straw. I already knew I was only "fresh meat" to him and when he was finished with me he was going to kick me to the curb. That was the end of him.

All I kept thinking about was one of those movies I had seen where people are getting high, and one person overdoses and the other people roll them up in the rug and dispose of the body. I knew that I couldn't do that. So we never spoke or saw each other again.

Smoking Cocaine

Snorting cocaine was not that bad. I really enjoyed the high it gave me, but I didn't like the way it made my nose run uncontrollably. It was embarrassing to me because it would always start running at the wrong time. One day my cousin Shelly came over with a lot of her friends. They needed a place to get high. They were hyper and excited about this cocaine, she said, "Girl this is some good stuff, it is hot off the boat." I had been refusing to smoke but this day I decided to try it. They had a whole lot of it and I figured what the heck.

When the pipe was passed to me I was afraid to hit it. They had to help me because I was scared to put the flame close to my face. I thought it might burn me or the glass pipe would explode and cause me to go blind. Shelly said, "Give it here girl you are so scary. Hit it, hit it, don't be scared. Now hold it, then blow it out slow!" I was sitting there holding it. Shelly said, "Dang girl for somebody who has never smoked before, you tried to smoke the who thing! Blow it out!" I began blowing it out real slow. At that moment, I had experienced a high like I had never, ever, ever, had before. I sat there totally enjoying the high for a moment. I said to myself, "Shoot, I like this stuff!" Before you knew it, it was my turn to hit again. They were moving really fast. I said to myself, "SIow down!" The more I hit, the more hyper I got too.

All of a sudden they grabbed their stuff and left. Shelly looked at me laughing and said, "Look at you, you so high! You like that don't you? I'll be back." I let them out and I sat there wondering, "Now what do I do with myself." I felt like cleaning or running or something. One thing I did know, from now on the cocaine I got would be going on a pipe. Every opportunity I got, I would freebase. I was even beginning to get interested in the cooking process. I begged my cousin to teach me. It was intriguing. It reminded me of the chemistry lab in college.

It took a lot of begging, but one night when Shelly came over she showed me how to cook. I asked a lot of questions and she didn't feel like answering them, but she did. After I watched her a few times I asked, "Can I cook the next one?" She said, "No you don't know what you're doing!" I told her, "Come on please let me do it! Please!" Of course she started fussing, all the while letting me cook a little bit. She could not teach me without raising her voice. I didn't care long as I got to do it. I did a really good job for my first time; the only thing was the rock had too much baking soda left in it. So I interrogated her as to why that happened so I wouldn't do it again. After several episodes like this, I became a master cook. I liked to cook and I loved to get high. It was a high that you can never reach again, but you sure would try. Freebasing affected everybody differently. I turned out to be one of the bad ones.

Chapter 6 Playing the Field

After my last serious relationship with Mr."D", I decided to just play the field. There were many guys that I met. They would get what they wanted and I would get what I wanted and we would go our separate ways. After all isn't that how you play the game?

I was meeting a lot of people and I was being invited to a lot of parties. One night this girl my sister and I knew was having a birthday party for her brother. I decided that I would go. When I arrived it was a nice party. There were a lot of family members there. I suppose that is why there were a lot of older people. No one was really dancing. They were sitting around mingling. I guess it wasn't that kind of party.

The DJ was playing all of the right music. Well, you know me! If I like the music, I'm going to dance. I would be the life of the party and would dance by myself if I had to. I finished a few drinks and I was feeling good. Practically all night long I danced by my self. I was on the dance floor having fun. Really having a good time. That is what I did no matter what. Even though I was dancing alone most of the time, it wasn't as if I was making a spectacle of myself. I guess the ones watching was enjoying seeing me dance. I know they wanted to dance but they were letting something hold them back. I used to be like that but not anymore. For me it was no holds bar. If I wanted to do it and I wasn't harming anyone else, then I did it.

I noticed an older gentlemen sitting all night long drinking, talking and looking. Unfortunately he never asked me to dance. When he got up to leave, he looked at me but said nothing. As he was walking through the house, speaking to people along the way, I watched him too. The host of the party walked him to the car. When she came back in the house she came right over to me and said, "Girl, all night he wanted to talk to you. He told me to give you his number." I took off running immediately to the front of the house to see if he was still in the driveway. He was cute and I couldn't let him get away.

He was an African-American male. He had a fair complexion; salt and pepper hair and he had hazel eyes. I just admired people with different color eyes. I thought to myself, "Because he is an older man, maybe he has good sense and knows how to treat a lady." So I went for it.

When I made it to the front of the house he was still in the driveway. I walked up to the window of his van. He rolled down the window and we began to talk. We exchanged phone numbers said good night and I went back inside the house and continued to have a good time. At the end of the night I wondered if he would really call me for a date or not. (Let's call him Ruben)

After a few days, he called me for a date. I was so excited. I said to myself, "Finally a mature man who seems to have it going on." I believe I was tired of dating men that had nothing but game and drama to offer. I was in my twenties and he was much older. I didn't care because I knew that I was mature. I felt or shall I say I knew that I could handle him. I thought, "Maybe he knows how to treat a nice girl like me!" On our first date he was quite impressive. (Mind you I am still married but separated from my husband)

Ruben picked me up and off we went. He fixed me a drink right there in his vehicle. It was fixed up. I felt like I was being wined and dined. I really liked our first date and I was looking forward to another one soon. I remember after about our second date he told me that he couldn't go out with me anymore because I was too nice of a girl and he didn't want to hurt me in any way. I couldn't imagine how in the world he was speaking of hurting me. I talked him into believing he wouldn't hurt me and that we could be together and it would be okay. After sitting and talking for long time, and doing a few other things, we became a pair.

Every time Ruben said he was coming to get me, he would come. He very seldom stood me up. If something happened he would almost always call. He wasn't into playing those silly games. He would take me around his friends, who were much older than I was. We would play cards and drink. It was just a few friends getting together to have a good time on the weekend. I could tell by the way they looked at me, they were wondering how he got a young girl like me. At the time we were dating I was thin and quite sexy and Chic. All eyes were on me. They would tell me all night long how good I looked and tease me about how I didn't need to be with an old man like him. By the time that I met this older man I was freebasing cocaine. He didn't know it thou. We drank and smoked a little weed together but that was the extent of it. Well, as you know, it doesn't take long before things get progressively worst.

At the time I met Ruben, I was living in the back house again. Even though I had a man now, I felt that I was still my own woman. I had a hard time with someone telling me what I could and couldn't do. I had been done wrong by so many guys in the past, my philosophy was, I would be as faithful to you as I could, but until you put a ring on my finger and we say “I do”, you don’t own me. You have no right to control my life. In the beginning he didn’t let me in on the secret of his wife and children but eventually it all came out. He told me they existed but he and his wife wasn’t a pair. Like I said, “He wasn’t my husband, he didn’t own me, and had no right to try and control me.” I had already been through enough guys to know this was all a big game. He was playing me and I was playing him. I had enough sense to know that even though we might really care a lot for each other, it would never really amount to anything.

After all, when he left me for the night I couldn’t check on him. I didn’t know where he was going and who he would be with. He knew how to reach me, and where to find me at any given time. I couldn’t go over to his house and I was never invited. So I knew better. Even though I knew he would never change his status and marry me, I chose to believe maybe just maybe he would. Maybe it was all of the drugs I was beginning to take at this time that was driving my emotions totally out of control.

While dating Ruben I was still working for the temporary agency and I was what you call a “functioning addict.” I was smoking more cocaine than Ruben could ever imagine. He had begun to get really curious about what I was doing. One day I told him. I also expressed to him freebasing is something he really shouldn’t get into. He wouldn’t leave well enough alone. He was so persistent, until one day I let him have a hit. The day that happened was the day Ruben and I made a huge mistake!

Now we were two demons on the loose. Even though he was smoking he wasn't as bad off as I was. Not yet anyway. I was getting worse by the day. Sometimes I stayed out all night smoking. Ruben searched for me and when he found me he would be sorely upset. He couldn't understand why I went all over town smoking and not stay at home. He didn't understand the game. I guess what made him really mad, I was supposed to be his lady and I was here and there smoking dope. That was making him look bad. It wasn't about him, it was all about me and what I wanted. I couldn't help or shall I say I couldn't prevent myself from doing what I was doing. This was the beginning of my demise.

Ruben needed to learn quickly if I couldn't control myself, he didn't have a chance. It wasn't going to happen no matter how much he tried; and boy did he try. What he would call defiant, I told him I was just being myself. My mom, husband, no one was able to make me do what they wanted me to do. Neither could anyone make me do what I should do, not even myself.

Ruben was supposed to be my man. I wasn't married to him. I was still married to my husband. He wasn't taking care of me, so I don't know what made him think he had the right to do what he was doing. He told me once that if he was my man, he needed to protect me. He needed to know what I was doing and where I was at all times. It all sounded good, but I knew better. He was trying to control me! Even though I tried to pretend I was happy, I was very sad and I knew I was addicted. I wanted to self-destruct. I wanted all of my problems to go away, but they compounded.

Don't Talk About Me

All of my life I had been talked about. Now I'm a grown woman doing my own thing. I felt whether I was doing right or wrong, as long as I wasn't hurting anyone else, I had a right to do it. One day I was out with my boyfriend, Ruben, and I stopped by mom's house. My mother and baby sister were there. While I was talking to my mother, my baby sister walked up and began talking about Ruben and me. Before I knew it, I had her bent over in a headlock. I was punching her in the face repeatedly like I was deranged. My mother and my sister were screaming, "Stop!" Mom was trying to get me to stop but I kept punching her. As she tried to lift her head, I caught a glimpse of bright red blood oozing down her face.

When I saw the blood, I snapped out of the rage and came back to myself. I thought, "Oh my God!" I let her go and immediately walked out the front door and headed straight to the car. Ruben asked me, "What's wrong?" I just shook my head and said "Nothing." I didn't want to talk about it because; I couldn't believe what I did to my dear, sweet, baby sister.

As we drove off, I kept asking myself, "What is wrong with you, why did you do that?" I was hurt because I just hurt someone else. I did it before I had time to think. I felt I was being controlled.

I did the same thing to my older sister at a family gathering. I was sitting at the dining room table and she was in the kitchen washing dishes. She began to talk about me. As I sat there listening I became more and more upset. I never said a word. I got up from the table and I walked in the kitchen where she was. I jumped on her. Sheila is a fighter too and she fought back. Her husband had to break us apart. I was beginning to feel like I was losing my mind.

There were two other episodes. One was with my sister, Santa, and the other was my mother's employee, Ella Mae. No matter what, it seem like every time I went to the laundromat and Ella was there, she would find something negative to say about me. Out of respect for her, I wouldn't say anything just endure the pain. I asked myself, "Why does she do this to me and I have done nothing to her?" This went on for years. On this particular day, I was all grown up now and I was on drugs really bad. She began to talk about me. Out of respect for her, I didn't put my hands on her, yet I cursed her out so bad she never did that to me again. My mother stood there in shock as I went on and on.

Afterwards, I felt really bad, but those drugs were turning me into a monster. If you hurt me in any way, you would catch the wrath of my rage and anger. Don't bother me and I won't bother you!

Nursing School

I was downtown LA on my way to work and someone handed me a flyer about a career college enrolling students. I thought, "This could be great opportunity for me to try and get back on the right road." I enrolled and started going to school. I was so excited and my family was excited for me also, especially my mother. She was telling everyone I was back in school. She was proud of me and I was proud of myself.

School was a challenge for me but I always liked a good challenge. I had to work hard but this was what I really liked to do. I loved business work and I loved nursing. Medical Administrative Assistance coupled with learning EEG, EKG and Phlebotomy was like having a combination of both of the things I liked. I knew I had found the answer for me to get a handle on things in life. I went shopping for my uniforms and my shoes after I enrolled.

I was doing exceptionally well. There was one other girl in class that was doing as well as I was. We were always competing with each other in a good way; we were quite fond of each other. We worked really hard at doing our very best. My studies did manage to slow me down a little with the drugs. I felt like I was making headway.

Now that I was in school, everyone seemed to be happy for me except Ruben. It seemed he was trying to make my life a living hell. He knew I had to study and go to school, but it didn't stop him from fussing and fighting with me all the time. I couldn't believe I had this man in my life that was obsessed with trying to control me. I continuously asked myself, "Why me?" "Why in the world do I have this older man in my life and I still can't have peace." When I started to date him I knew he would be the answer! Unfortunately, I was beginning to believe this wasn't going to work either.

I had to take a test and I was so upset, even the teacher noticed. She called me over to her desk and asked me what was going on. When I explained to her, I started to cry uncontrollably. I cried my heart out and told her about Ruben and all he was doing to me. She told me I deserved better and I should leave him.

All of the things I needed to do sounded simple, but for me they were very difficult. I said to myself "Yeah I hear you talking but you don't have a clue as to what you are suggesting." I stopped crying, took the test and did very well. This same thing went on day after day. There were times he didn't want me to go to school but I pressed on anyway.

I had on my bright white uniform. It was fresh and clean. I was on my way to school and decided to go in the opposite direction. Instead I went to the dope house. I wanted to get a little hit before I went to school. This wasn't one of my regular spots. I didn't know these people very well. I knocked on the door and a guy answered and let me inside. After I purchased a small amount, I asked, "Can I smoke it right quick because I have to go to school?" He said, "Okay." As he was setting up everything for me and another customer, there was a loud banging at the front door! Then one of the windows was hit! Then another window on the side of the house was hit! Then there was a loud bang at the kitchen window where we were standing! I was so scared I didn't move! Everyone one was running around. I just stood in the kitchen frozen in place with a plate of cocaine in my hand. Suddenly a guy came up to me and put a big silver gun to my head and yelled, "PUT IT DOWN ON THE COUNTER NOW!!" My first thought after being scared to death was, I didn't even get to hit this stuff!

It was a raid! Apparently the police had been watching the house. Why did this have to happen when I was in the house? They were looking everywhere for dope. They asked me and I told them, "I don't know anything. I just got here and this is my first time coming over here." Those police handcuffed me and put me in the back of the car. I was crying and trying to tell them I was on my way to school. The officer said, "You should have gone to school instead of coming over here. Now we have to take you to jail!"

They told me, "Because this is your first time, they will book you and let you go. Then you will have to come back to court and see the judge." I guess the time I went to jail for stealing from JC Penney didn't count. That was good for me! I was glad when they said to me, "You can go now!" Jail was the place I tried to avoid at all cost! I told myself, "Go to school and stay until you finish!

I met this really nice girl in class. We hit it off because we had an outside interest. I found out she liked to get high. Occasionally I would go to her house to study and smoke a little bit.

One day when I was at her house, somehow and some way, Ruben showed up at her door asking for me. I told her, "Tell him I not here!" Well, that didn't work. When she opened the door he just walked on in. She was fussing and cursing because she couldn't believe how aggressive he was. As she was loud talking him, he was looking around trying to find me. He said, "I saw her come in, I know she's here." The apartment wasn't that big and it didn't take him long to find me in one of her closets.

As he swung the door open, I knew it wasn't going to be pretty. He tried to grab me out of the closet, I resisted, only making matters worse. I managed to snatch away from him the first time, but he grabbed me again. He grabbed me in the face and cut me on the side of my eye. My eye started watering and I was very upset. I was yelling, screaming and fighting and he was really trying to calm me down. He didn't want to alarm the neighbors because they might call the police.

Stupid me! I left with him again. I didn't want my friend to get in trouble, and besides, I knew he wasn't going to leave her place without me. All the way home I had to hear a lecture. When I went to school I knew my friend was going to have a few choice words for me.

The next day my friend politely told me, I was no longer welcome at her house. She thought Ruben was insane and she said, "The next time he does something like this I will find someone to put a hurting on him." I was so embarrassed. It was episodes like this that I had to endure all the time.

August 5, 1983, was our graduation. Oh yes! I did manage to graduate and I was second in my class. My competitor beat me by a few points. That was okay; I still did very, very well. I did outstanding considering my circumstances. I was proud of myself because I had finally accomplished something. I remember graduation day just like it was yesterday. My parents were on the front row sitting there ever so proudly, as they watched their troubled child finally achieve something. It was such a lovely day. Believe it or not, they had me on the program to do the welcome. I thought I was on my way to a happy lifestyle! I was excited, but I still had work to do.

I was told I had to study to go before the board. I also needed to prepare for interviews. Immediately I began to panic. As soon as she said, "Test for the board," I knew I didn't want to do that and I procrastinated. My instructor was a nice lady who was serious about us succeeding and doing well. Determined to help me in any way she could, she even set up an interview for me. From the time I learned the date of the interview up until the actual day, I tortured myself. I thought, "Will they like me? Will I answer all of the questions right? Will I have to take any test?" I was so stressed that on the day of the interview I didn't go. I could see myself doing the job, but I couldn't make myself go to the interview. I watched the clock until I knew that it was too late to go. My instructor called me and asked why I didn't go and I told her some sort of lie. I really don't think she believed me. I didn't go to the board either. Yes, my parents were very disappointed with me and I was equally disgusted with myself. Of course, I had to hear Ruben say, "I told you so."

Out of all my classes my favorite was Phlebotomy. I loved drawing blood. I enjoyed it so much because it was like an art. You had to do it just right in order for it to work and not hurt the patient. Unfortunately, I let all that knowledge and skill go unused. I still have the portfolio I made in the class. I guess it serves as a reminder that I really do have potential.

Potential

Speaking of potential, I met a man (let's call him Howard) who was a dope dealer/user and he told me I had potential. He was a friend of my cousin Shelly. He would come by the house sometimes to prepare his cocaine and marijuana, or he would drop by to smoke a little bit and talk. One day he asked, "If I give you some cocaine, do you think you could sell it and not smoke it all up?" Because I knew I was good at selling, I told him, "Yes" immediately. I figured I could sell for him, and smoke for free. This way I would still be saving myself money. He came by several times to freebase and discuss business. I had what it took to be a good dealer, so he thought! Well the day finally came. He brought the cocaine and everything I needed. There was only one thing I must not do, tell Shelly, his girlfriend. He said, "If she finds out, she's gonna try and get it from you and smoke it all up." I vowed not to tell her.

I was in business now! Right away Shelly came by to freebase. Because I had my own place, people would always stop by and do their drugs. It was really good for me so I made sure I stayed stocked with a pipe, some rum, and a lighter. You see, as a rule, you always had to give a cut to the house! When she smoked all she had, she asked me to give her some of mine. I told her, "I don't have anything." She said, "I know Howard gave you some cocaine to sell, so go get it!" After going back and forth for what seemed like forever, she got mad and left! Because I was so stressed out, I decided to smoke a little bit of it. I figured the little bit I smoked would basically be my profit after the sales anyway.

This saga went on and on. Howard called from time to time and asked how I was doing. He told me he would let me know when he was coming by to pick up the money. He asked if my cousin was harassing me. I told him, "Yes, but I didn't let her have anything." The day came when he was going to come by and make a pick up. I was smoking cocaine and trying to figure out what I was going to tell him. I didn't have all of the money and the cocaine was just about gone.

I had smoked a lot of it. I smoked my portion and then some. I knew he was going to be furious. I imagined him literally knocking my head off. If he did I would have deserved it. I was so nervous.

The moment finally came; there was a knock at the door. I had fixed myself up and I tried to look my very best. When I opened the door he was standing there smiling like he always would and asked me, "What's up?" I told him, "Nothing, come on in." He came in, sat down and we began to talk. I thought, "Please just keep on shooting the breeze. Don't ask me about the cocaine, please just don't ask!"

He asked me for the money. After counting it he asked, "Is this all the money you have? Where's the rest of the stuff? Is this it?" I asked myself, "How in the world could I tell him I don't have any left?

What is he going to do to me when he finds out I smoked it all? How was I going to tell him I smoked all of that dope by myself?"

Howard was really upset. He sat there for a moment and then he asked, "Do you have a pipe and some rum?" He made a sarcastic remark, "I bet you do!" I told him, "Yes." By the time I got back with the equipment, my table was full of cocaine! As he began smoking, I just sat there and watched. After he took a few hits, he passed the pipe to me. I wasn't sure if I should hit it or not! I thought, "Is he going to slap the pipe out of my hand or what?" I was one scared sister. Not too scared to take a hit though! When it came to freebasing, I could never get enough. I reached for the pipe and I hit it and I passed it back to him.

Howard began telling me I had made a big mistake. I told him how I tried to do the right thing, but I lost control and I messed up. He went on to tell me how disappointed he was with me and how I had let him down. To my dismay after much scolding he said, "Because I think you have potential, I'm gonna give you some more and give you another chance." I didn't know if I should take it or not. After thinking for a minute or two, I said, "I... maybe I shouldn't take anymore." He said, "You have potential and I know you can do it. So I'm gonna take another chance. Give you some dope to work with."

I blew that too. I just couldn't do right. To make matters worse, this time when my cousin asked if

Howard had given me some cocaine, I told her yes. She said, "I knew he was giving you some, how could you do this me?" I guess I got tired of all of the begging and besides I was messing the stuff up again! We both messed up this time. We smoked it up together. To her, it really didn't mean anything. I guess she felt she was entitled to it. I, on the other hand, felt like a total failure.

This time when Howard came by, he brought Shelly with him. We were all at my house together and they started arguing over what was going on. I couldn't take it anymore. I just wanted everyone to get along. Besides I was so upset with myself because I had failed again. I turned around as they were standing there in my house arguing and walked out the door. I didn't say a word. I walked up the driveway and down the street. I walked all the way to Adams Boulevard. I started crossing the street. Someone grabbed me and told me to get out of the street. It wasn't until then that I realized what I was doing. I was about to get hit by some cars. I remember hearing horns blowing. I guess I was walking in a daze or something. Howard asked, "What's wrong with you?" and I told him, "I don't know?" He took me back home and then they left. All I know is I couldn't stand to hear them arguing and fussing.

Howard didn't give me any more cocaine to sell for him but we did continue to kick it together. He would often come by to take care of his business. If

Howard was there, I didn't have to worry. There was going to be more cocaine than I could ever dream of smoking. He was very generous too. It was always a pleasure to know he was stopping by! He was what we classified as a "Roller."

Because I didn't follow through after graduating from the Career College, I was still working for the banks through the temp agency. Faithfully I would go to work Monday –Friday. I started to miss work when I got my paycheck. I could no longer wait until I got off work to get high. The temp agency I was working for called me into the office one day and asked me why I never showed back up for work on Friday once I received my paycheck. I told them some kind of a lie and they warned me if it didn't stop they were going to have to let me go. I really did like working for them and they really liked me too. I was always shown favor by them. If a really good job came up at a bank they would always call me first. Don't get me wrong, I was using drugs but I was a darn good, hard worker.

I was beginning to really get addicted to the dope I was smoking and that wasn't good. I was smoking weed and sometimes I would lace the weed with cocaine. I would work sometimes for twelve hours. I would work overtime and weekends. It didn't matter to me. Once I got to work, they knew that they could always count on me to be there for as long as they needed.

Sleeping on the Job

At work I was extremely tired. I decided to take a nap while I was on my break. I worked the second shift. I ended up sleeping my entire shift, only to be awakened by the morning supervisor. I had slept through the night in the bathroom lounge. The next day I had to answer for doing such an unthinkable thing. I didn't realize I was a functioning addict on the way to destruction. All of my wrongdoing was slowly but surely catching up with me. I made really good money doing what I was doing but it was all going up in a puff of smoke.

The temp agency was constantly finding me work, but I was beginning to become a no- show. Little did they know I wasn't working all of the hours requested of me. I figured I could get away with adding a few hours I didn't work and no one would notice. They never asked me any questions. I simply filled out my time card and they issued me a check.

After several times doing this, I went to pick up my check and the secretary called me into the office and said, "What's going on with you?" I said, "Nothing, why do you ask?" She said, "I found out that you are not working all of the hours you are claiming on your time card." I looked at her like I had just seen a ghost. I knew I was going to jail! Again she asked, "What is going on with you? Why are you doing this? Do you realize what kind of trouble you are getting yourself into?"

I just opened up then. I thought I would fall on the mercy seat. I didn't want to go to jail for falsification, so I told her everything. She was very understanding. She told me she too had been a drug addict in her past life. She said, "I am going to have to let you go! If the owner finds out, he would probably bring charges against you. Besides he is so fond of you. He really trusted you!" I sat there and cried because I did have a wonderful relationship with the owner. I knew I had let him and his company down. I knew if he found out, he would be very disappointed with me and neither she nor I wanted him to know.

I left that agency, never to return again. I was so upset with myself. Those people really trusted me, and they treated me like a professional. Once again, I blew it. How come I couldn't do right? Why did I manage to keep screwing everything up in my life? Now I had to find another job because I had to support my drug habit. I was really trying to incorporate working and using! It was becoming more and more difficult!

I had to find means of generating cash to get high. I began doing the unthinkable. I would sleep around with people I hardly knew or didn't know at all. As long as they were willing to give me money or drugs I would have sex with them. Because I wasn't used to this type of behavior, it was very difficult to do.

The worst thing about doing it is, while your body is going through the motions, your emotions are being tortured. It had an indescribable effect on my mind!

Chapter 7
Pregnant

I had been out smoking cocaine all day and was extremely exhausted. I came home to my apartment and passed out on the couch. In the middle of the night I had to get up and go to the bathroom. On my way I looked at myself in the huge mirror that was leaning on the wall in the living room. I noticed my stomach was poking out. I had on a straight dress, which we called a "shift"; this type of a dress would fit you smug like a glove. You had to have a nice shape for this dress to look right. I was about a size eight with a flat stomach. After taking a look at myself I had to back up and look again. I couldn't believe what I was seeing. My stomach looked like I was about four months pregnant. I screamed, "Oh My God, what is wrong with my stomach?" When I laid down my stomach was flat. When I got up my stomach was protruding. I was concerned and afraid because I couldn't imagine what was wrong with my belly. What happened to make my stomach grow like this in a matter of hours? I was scared, and pregnancy was the furthest thing from my mind.

I was bewildered, but because I was so tired, I just laid back down. While I was trying to figure out what was wrong with me, I fell fast asleep.

I found out I was pregnant. I can't remember how many months I was, but I was pretty far along. When I went to the doctor they wanted to know why I waited so long. I had to start prenatal vitamins right away.

What was I going to do with a baby? I already had a son I wasn't properly taking care of. I was using drugs on a regular basis, drinking alcohol, smoking cigarettes, weed, and Cocaine; and experimenting with other drugs. I was partying and living a wild life. I knew the repercussions of the life I had been living. I considered once again having an abortion. Once my friends and family found out, they highly recommended that I get an abortion also. They told me due to all of the different drugs I was using; my baby would be retarded, severely handicapped or still born. It really put a lot on my mind. By me once wanting to become an RN, I somewhat knew the danger I was putting the baby in and I knew I would be taking a chance on having a good healthy baby. I took their advice and I went to an abortion clinic.

It really brought back memories of the first time I murdered my baby. I didn't like killing my babies. I was still having nightmares of the first baby I killed back in 1975. It was a horrible thing I had done and here I was considering it again. I knew what I was about to do wasn't right, but I didn't stop proceeding to the clinic. I walked into the clinic and signed in. The receptionist asked me for my medical card and I gave it to her and took a seat. In no time at all the receptionist called me back up to the window and told me my medical card wasn't good. I asked her what she meant. There should be nothing wrong with the card. She said, "It is denied! We can't proceed unless you want to pay cash!" I had the cash to get it done but I wasn't going to take my dope money to get an abortion. I had been using my card without any problems, but today, some reason it was rejected.

Even though the card was denied and I couldn't get an abortion, I had a plan. I knew if I continued on with this pregnancy the way I had been living, there would be no way the baby would survive. I would end up having a miscarriage or still born baby. That's it! I will kill the baby in the womb. This will be a little different than having an abortion, but it will be okay.

Being pregnant for so long and not knowing is still a mystery to me. People couldn't believe that I was smoking and drinking while I was pregnant. I was a pretty pathetic individual, now that I think about it.

Sometimes I would get so sick. I would begin to dry heave. It would be horrible! They had to call the paramedics. My family was really getting sick and tired of the madness and me.

One morning when I awoke I didn't get up right away. I rested in bed meditating and thinking about all I had to do. I had a doctor's appointment that day. The baby had been very active in the past but this particular morning the baby wasn't moving. I became nervous and scared. I began to tap on one side of my belly to see if I could wake the baby up. There was no movement! I tapped on the other side, still no movement. I began to panic. I tapped and I tapped, and still no movement. My mind began to race. Has the baby died inside of me? "This is what you wanted isn't it?" I asked myself. You wanted for the baby to die so you wouldn't have to deal with a retarded or sickly baby! Isn't it? Isn't It?" I became scared and started to cry.

I couldn't stand the thought of this baby being dead on the inside of my body. Even though this was my plan, now that it seemed to be happening, I wanted to change my mind. I really wanted to change my mind. I cried and I cried out to God, "Please save this baby God, please don't let my baby die! I DON'T WANT THIS BABY TO DIE! PLEASE GOD DON'T LET MY BABY DIE". I cried and I cried and I cried. What seemed like hours were only minutes. I felt a jolt in my belly. I said to myself, "What's that?" Then it jolted again,

I yelled, "Oh my God, my baby! My baby! Thank you God my baby is Alive." Its alive, Thank you Jesus my baby is alive! I was so relieved to know that I had not killed this baby in my womb and that it was alive. What a relief! I thanked God for my baby being alive.

I finally got out of bed and prepared myself to go to the doctor. On that day I had a newfound respect for what was inside me. I was relieved I had not killed this baby. Some might wonder why I was happy the baby was still alive by the way I was living, but even though I kept on smoking drugs, and barely eating and taking care of myself like a pregnant woman should, I really was glad the baby was alive. I was still addicted and I was glad I was having a baby even though this wasn't a planned pregnancy.

The Time has Finally Arrived

As much as I wanted to be a good pregnant mother, I wasn't because I was still addicted. No matter how much I told myself I needed to stop doing drugs, it didn't matter because I kept doing it anyway. It was as if I was powerless. I continued to freebase cocaine, drink Alcohol, smoke cigarettes and marijuana, and continued to eat sporadically. When I did eat, it would make my heart race and I got sick.

One night I purchased a large quantity of cocaine and I smoked quite a bit. I smoked all night into the early morning. I decided to lie down. After smoking as much as I did, it was very difficult to fall asleep. I was "wired for sound" and my hearing became very keen and I was paranoid.

Sometime during the early morning I finally drifted off to sleep and before I knew it the sun was gleaming through the curtain on the window. I had to go to the bathroom really, really bad. I jumped out of the bed and rushed to the bathroom. Suddenly I began to feel warm water running down my leg. I said to myself, "I am peeing on myself." I tightened up the muscles in an effort to stop the flow, only to discover I had no control. I really had to go to the bathroom, but the flow wouldn't stop. I didn't know what to do.

I remembered a conversation my mother and I had just the other day. We discussed what happens when your water bag bursts. When I had my son they had to break my water so this was a new experience. That's it! My water bag had burst! What do I do now? I decided to get a towel and put it between my legs. I still had to use the bathroom, but was it safe to do so? I had no idea and was alone in my upstairs apartment. I didn't have a telephone to call any one.

As I gathered my thoughts, I made a decision to use the bathroom. After I did that, everything was still okay. When I was in high school I was preparing myself to be an RN and some of the things I learned were beginning to come back to me. "Oh my GOD", I screamed, "What in the world am I going to do?" OH no! Oh My GOD! NO not now!" In the midst of everything that had just happened, I forgot I had been freebasing cocaine all night long, and now it was time to have the baby. My first thoughts were that I was going to give birth to the baby and the baby was going to be taken away, and I was going to go to jail. I remember hearing if a child was born and if drugs were found in the baby's system, the mother would go to jail. I was terrified.

The time had finally come and I had to give birth, but I didn't want to. Of all days, why the morning after smoking all that cocaine? I knew I had smoked too much for it to go undetected.

I got dressed so I could go down stairs to use my neighbor's phone to call my sister. I wobbled down the stairs very slowly, with this towel still between my legs. When I finally made it to the door, I leaned on the big black iron security door and began to knock. Finally I heard, "What do you want?" It was my neighbor's son yelling at me. I didn't know that he would be there. Not that it really mattered today anyway. When I first moved in the building, everyone liked me until they found out I was a drug addict. No one seemed to care for me anymore. I could only imagine what he must have been thinking of me at that moment. What could I possible need with his mother?

Trying to hold back the tears, I quietly said to him, "I need to call my sister to come and take me to the hospital. My water bag has broken and I am about to have the baby." Immediately he changed his tone, ran and got the phone for me to use. He said, "What's the number?" I told him and he dialed it for me, and handed me the phone.

"Hello, hello Santa. I think it is time to have the baby, my water bag has just broke," I said. She said, "Where are you at?" I said, "I am at home." She said, "I am own my way!" I said, "Okay." I gave the phone back to the young man who appeared to be very concerned for me at this point. I thanked him. He said, "Are you going to be okay?" I told him, "Yes, my sister is on her way". He said, "Okay".

Very slowly I began walking back up the stairs to my apartment, still trying to hold the towel between my legs. It was very difficult. I sat on the couch and waited for my sister to arrive. It took her about an hour to come, but it seemed more like four hours.

As I was sitting on the couch I heard noise and rumbling. It was Santa coming up the stairs and down the walkway. When I opened the door she looked scared. It was a long ride to the hospital. I lived on one side of Los Angeles and the hospital was across town in Fox Hills. We had to take the street route all the way there. The closer we got to the hospital, the more nervous I became. I had to face whatever was going to happen to me.

After being admitted into the hospital, they put me in a room and began working on me. I know I must have had a look on my face that was indescribable. I was scared for my life, but there wasn't anything left to do but have the baby. My sister didn't leave my side. She stayed there the entire time. I was grateful for that. She called my mother and other sisters. It was no secret, they all knew I was on drugs and they were concerned.

Even though my water bag had broken, they still had to induce my labor. With my first son I had natural childbirth, but I believe being induced was more painful. It hurt so much even being full of cocaine. I remember telling my sister to ask the nurse if I could have something for the pain. The nurse came in the room and told me what she could give me. I didn't care as long as it worked! I immediately began to feel better. I felt so good I took a nap. The pain woke me up. It had started again. I was in as much pain as I was before they gave me the medicine.

I asked Santa to find the nurse again. When the nurse came in the room she said, "Ma'am we just gave you medicine and we cannot give you anymore right now." I looked at her and began to cry. The pain was horrific! With all of the cocaine I smoked hours ago, I was surprised at the pain I was feeling. I was in so much pain I could just scream! That is just what I did. I screamed, and screamed, and screamed! I screamed so much until one of the nurses came into the room and said in a very harsh tone, "Out of all of the woman in the hospital having babies, you are the only one making all of this noise. Please stop!"

I looked at the nurse as she was leaving my room and I told her, "I am the only Sha in the hospital, and if I needed to scream I was going to scream!" My sister looked at me in total disbelief. The nurse was so insensitive to me. She had no idea how much pain I was in. I wished someone would put me out of my misery. That's pretty much how I had been feeling every day for the past few years.

Now I am hurting and upset. My sister really tried to calm me down. I should have been quiet and not draw any attention to myself, knowing what was flowing through my veins! After much agony, I felt it was time. The nurse came into the room to check on me and I told her I thought it was time and she told me she had just checked me and I still had a ways to go. I told her, "No I think it was time!" She walked out of the room. I told my sister, "Go get someone else because something is going on and I think it's time." I believe that I was actually yelling and pushing at the same time. My sister wasn't gone long before she came back with another nurse. I said, "I think the baby is coming". She said, "Okay let me take a look and see what is going on." She walked to the foot of my bed, pulled up the covers and then she began to speak very stern to me. "Stop pushing, don't push any more, you are right the baby is coming and we need to get you to the delivery room right away." She left the room swiftly. I knew it, I knew it, I knew it was time!

It was finally time for me to deliver and I was a nervous wreck about the outcome of it all. I didn't know what to expect, but I had a pretty good idea. Considering the circumstances, it wasn't going to be good. I was so petrified!

The Delivery

Suddenly people came rushing into my room. "Ms. Jackson," the nurse said, "It is time for us to take you to the delivery room." They asked my sister, "Are you going to be in the delivery room?" She said, "Yes." "Then you need to put on the white suit", she said. Everything was set up, and as usual, it was very cold in there. They put my legs in the stirrups and did what they had to do. I pushed and screamed and huffed and puffed until the next thing I knew the baby was out and I could hear it crying. Now I am afraid of the unknown. I didn't know what they were going to do when they found out I had drugs in my system. What kind of "crack baby" is this going to be?

I was relieved to hear the baby make a sound. Finally I heard the doctor say, "It's a girl" I said, "A girl," happy and relieved that it was finally over. I just wanted to go to sleep. Then I thought again, "Oh my God, Santa, check the baby's fingers and toes, check the fingers and toes." She said, "Okay." I reiterated again check the fingers and toes now! After she checked, she quietly and calmly told me, "The baby has ten fingers and ten toes." I smiled and sighed with relief.

At that point, I wanted to see her. I really wanted to see her bad. Finally they handed her to me. As they lowered the baby down, I was in total shock when I saw her face. My complexion is described as "Dark chocolate" and this baby girl's complexion was like "White chocolate!" When I looked at her hair, there wasn't a curl anywhere. Her hair stood straight up like a porcupine. As I looked at her and she at me, all I could say was, "THANK YOU LORD! YOU SAVED MY BABY! THANK YOU!" I held on to her for as long as they let me. She was a beautiful baby girl with no noticeable birth defects. For that I was eternally grateful to my God.

After a moment they came and took her from me and assured me I would be getting her back soon. I said to myself, "Yea right, I know that after you take her and draw blood, all hell is going to break loose." As much as I wanted to lie there and fret about the whole situation, I was so tired I went to sleep.

I woke up to the sound of a nurse calling my name. I was now in a room with another woman who had just had a baby. They came into the room to check on me. I was surprised I was still in the hospital. I said to myself, "They must not have found out yet." When the nurse was getting ready to walk out of the room I asked her if she would bring my baby. I had not seen her in a while because I had been sleeping. This would also be my way of seeing if the baby was still in the hospital or if she had been taken somewhere. The nurse told me, "Sure I can go and check and see if it is okay to bring her to you right now." I said, "Okay." In the meantime, I am hoping and praying that they weren't going to come back in my room with the police.

Before I knew it, they were bringing by beautiful bundle of joy to me. My sister, Santa, was still right there with me. I didn't want to be there by myself in case they decided to come and get me in the middle of the night and take me to jail.

The nurse asked if I wanted the baby to stay the night. I told her, "Yes." Believe it or not no one bothered us all night. Not until early the next morning. The nurse said they needed to take the baby out for a moment and when they were done they would bring her back. Every time someone came into my room, I thought they were coming to get me and take me to jail. I was a nervous wreck!

When my oldest sister came to visit me she stopped by the nursery to see the baby first and she had jokes by the time she got to my room. She walked in the room and said, "I believe they gave you the wrong baby. That baby is too light to be your baby. Are you sure that baby belongs to you?" I told her, "Yes, it's my baby, and thank God Santa witnessed the birth." If she had not been there, I might have wondered the same thing.

Before I knew it, I was being dismissed from the hospital. I couldn't understand how they did not know I had drugs in my system? How did the drugs in the baby go undetected? How did I manage to slide by on this one? I knew it was by the grace of God!

Grace

Because of God's grace, I delivered a healthy baby girl and wasn't taken to jail for drug abuse and endangering my child. She had no birth defects and had all her limbs and organs functioning normally. It was truly God's grace! As I thought about how good the Lord had been to my baby and me, I gave her a middle name of "Grace". I later added "Santa" after my sister who was there with me. "Grace Santa" would be the middle name. Both helped me make it through that day and I was eternally grateful. I filled out my paper work and on the birth certificate I put down Ruben as the father since I was dating him at the time. His complexion is what we describe as "high yellow" so maybe that explains why she was so fair! "Maybe?" I decided to deal with that later. He wasn't there anyway!

Chapter 8
Delivered...So I Thought

Where was Ruben and why wasn't he there with me? Good question! When we left the hospital the first stop was my momma's house. She had not seen the baby.

Momma said the same thing, "Oh, she is so light!" At that moment, I made up in my mind that whenever I took my baby out in public, I was going to make sure I had her birth certificate with me. I didn't want anyone thinking I had stolen a baby. No joke, I carried the birth certificate with me everywhere I went. I decided to stay at my mom's house because it would be lonely at my apartment. She didn't mind and neither did my dad.

Everyday mom went to work at the laundromat except on Sundays. I stayed home with the baby. I don't remember having a baby shower for "Grace," but I had a lot of beautiful clothes for her. People were very generous in their giving and Grace had many cute outfits. I would change her clothes three times a day. During the day I kept the house clean, did a little cooking, and took care of my babies. Well, Michael wasn't a baby any more. He was eight years old at the time.

When I moved into my own apartment, my son stayed at my mother's house because he was attending the school right around the corner. It was working out really nice with my being there. I knew Jr. was glad I was there every day with him. I wasn't sure how he felt about Grace. It appeared as if he took to her very well. He would hold her and play with her all the time. He kissed all over her whenever he got the chance. He loved his baby sister. It was great! I had the whole day to myself, just the baby and me.

When I delivered Grace, it was as if God delivered me. I no longer had a desire to use drugs. No desire. The thrill was gone. I must admit, it felt good not being driven by the demon of drug addiction. I started going back to church and life was good to me again. I know people were talking about me, but I didn't care what they said. I was alive and well and I had two wonderful children to love.

I seldom went to my apartment, but I continued to pay the rent. I saw Ruben occasionally because we were not really dating. My ex-husband, well he was still my husband but we were still unofficially separated. Those were the stupid lies that I told myself knowing I was still a married woman.

I wasn't living with my husband and I was seeing who ever I wanted and he was doing the same. I was living life like a single lady. I was committing adultery and so was he. I guess we didn't really care. One day when my husband came to my mother's house, someone invited him to go in the room and see the baby. He initially declined. Finally they encouraged him to look at her. I remember him coming into the room walking slowly. Grace was lying on the bed looking adorable as always. He approached slowly while putting his hands behind his back. He walked up to the bed and leaned over her as if to pick her up, but didn't. After he took a long hard look at her, he walked away saying, " I will never pick her up!" I asked him why and he angrily said, "I will never pick her up!" and he swiftly left the house. Shortly thereafter my mother had him changing her diapers and everything else.

On occasion I would talk to my so-called boyfriend, Ruben. For some reason we just didn't get along, but we tried so hard to. I can't remember what he did to me, but whatever it was, it upset me as usual. I was so angry with him! I talked myself into going back to my apartment with the baby. Everyone asked me why I was going home, and I gave some lame excuse. Because of the anger I had towards Ruben, I decided to return to what made me happy. I started using drugs again. I was right where I left off six months ago. I didn't take my son with me because he was still going to school around the corner from my mom's house. I had limitations now because of the baby. I couldn't run the street like I used to, but I sure tried. When I got my county check (welfare) I was off to the races.

One time I went to the jungle (that is what they called this part of town) in the middle of the night to buy some cocaine. It was cold outside. I bundled the baby up in her car seat and took her with me. The jungle was located in Baldwin Hills, California and is in Los Angeles off Labrea Boulevard. It was a bad place to be during this era. I left the baby in the back seat of the car while I ran in the apartment to score (make a purchase). I had to drive across town to get back home. After all of that was gone, I jumped in the car and went back over there and scored again. I know you are wondering why I didn't get all I was going to get when I went the first time. Addicts don't think like that. We always mean to do better. I told myself I was only going to do a certain amount and that would be it, but once you get started, you can't stop. At least I couldn't. Not as long as I had money, and when I ran out of money, I would sit and meditate on ways to get more money. Then I could score and get high again. It was a vicious cycle.

Baby for Collateral

On night I went to score and I took the baby in the house with me. Everyone just adored her. While they were admiring her I decided to freebase there.

I smoked until all my stuff was gone. Other people were still smoking and they were encouraging me to leave and take the baby home. I wanted more so bad, I asked the guy who lived there if I could smoke some cocaine on credit. I told him I would leave the baby there until I came back with his money. Why did I say that? I never will forget it. He got so mad at me. He began cursing me out, picked up my baby and handed her to me. He almost pushed us down the stairs! He said, "Get out and you better not come back here again!" I was so embarrassed! I began to cry! I put the baby in the car and drove away.

I drove around trying to find something to get into. Finding nothing, I went back to my apartment and went to sleep. I couldn't believe I tried to leave my baby as collateral in a dope house! How could I even think of leaving her with strangers? That is how this sickness was for me. There were days when I was totally out of control.

Early one morning, I didn't have any money, but I had a strong urge to freebase. I took a look around my apartment and decided to sell some of my furniture. I took apart my favorite bamboo swing chair that was hooked onto a black heavy-duty iron hanger and put it in my car and drove up and down the street.

I came upon this house where a woman and her son were outside. I asked her, "Would you be interested in buying this chair?" She said, "How much do you want for it?" I can't remember what I ended up selling the chair for, but it was far less than what I had paid for it. As a matter of fact, she bought several of the pieces I had for sell.

All of these items I had worked really hard for and put them on layaway until I could get them out. Among the other items sold were a mirrored cube table, and a silver chrome and glass étagère. When the lady agreed to buy the other items, I asked her, "Can I leave my baby here until I came back? The items are big and heavy, and I will need all of the space I have in the car!" She solemnly said, "Yes." Her son stood there looking at me saying nothing. I could only imagine what he was thinking about me.

The lady paid me for the chair and then for the other items when I returned. I left the baby and the diaper bag just in case she needed it before I returned. I figured before I went and got the other items, I would score, take me a hit, and then get to work.

In my mind the process didn't seem like it was going to take very long. One thing led to another, and it was late in the evening when I went back to pick up the baby.

Of course, this lady was furious with me! I guess she said to herself, "I don't even know who this woman is and I have no way of getting in touch with her." She was very upset, but she still agreed to buy the items I had. We made the exchange and very few words were said.

Grace was still in her carrier on the floor screaming, and she was soaking wet. I wanted to change her diaper before I left the ladies' house, but she wouldn't allow me to do so. She just wanted me out of her house. I told her I was sorry and I took the baby and the money and left. I never will forget the look on her son's face as I picked up my crying baby and left. He was a tall handsome young man about in his mid twenties. He looked at me with disgust in his eyes, but he never said a word. Walking to the car, once again I felt like the worst mother in the world. I asked myself, "How in the world could you possibly leave your newborn baby with total, total strangers?"

I didn't know anything about these people at all. When I got in the car, and I picked up Grace, all of her clothes and socks were soaked. Even her long black silky hair was soaked from the accumulation of tears around her neck that she had shed ALL DAY LONG! I felt horrible! I just held her in my arms and told her I was so sorry for leaving her there for so long. I couldn't understand why they didn't at least change her diaper? She was so hungry. They didn't even give her a bottle. I guess they just let her lie there and cry. She was wet and full of tears and I was full of tears too. I knew it was time for me to take Grace and go home. When I walked into my apartment and saw almost all of my furniture gone, I felt lower than a rat in a gutter! Just the thought of re-living it brings me back shame. I remember asking myself, "What is wrong with me?" Then I began to feel worthless. By feeling worthless, I wanted to do one thing! Get some more cocaine, get high, in hopes to self-destruct. I went out and I got some more drugs. When I came back to the apartment, I immediately started getting high. I didn't even take the baby out of the car seat. I just put it on the bed and went in the bathroom and started smoking. Back and forth I would go. I was mad, I was angry, I was sick and I didn't like myself very much.

Because I was so high, I was very paranoid. Suddenly, I heard a knock on the door but I wouldn't open it. They left and then they came back, but I still wouldn't open it. I didn't even go to the peephole and try to see who it was. I didn't care and I didn't want to be bothered with anyone. Finally they left. Later I learned it was my husband and he had been sent to check on me because my family had not heard from me in a while.

In the meantime as I kept smoking, the apartment filled up with smoke. I had to continuously fan the smoke alarm so it wouldn't go off. I didn't want to open the window because the smell would go outside and I was afraid someone would call the police.

Someone else came to the door, only this time they were banging like the police. I was curious, so I tip toed to the door, and looked through the peephole to see who it was. It was Ruben. I let him in because I knew he would cause a scene and I didn't want the manager to come outside. My apartment was right next to hers.

He came in asking me several questions. When I am getting high, I don't want to be bothered with answering questions. Of course I didn't answer him. I just wanted to keep on smoking. Besides, the baby was crying and getting on my nerves. I couldn't get her to stop crying. He took a couple of hits off the pipe, and then picked her up out of the car seat. He walked with her, and bounced her, and I just kept on getting high.

I was more concerned that the neighbors would hear her crying and call the police. They really didn't like me anyway. After a little while, he suggested we leave because Grace wouldn't stop crying. Of course, I didn't want to stop smoking but the crying was beginning to get on my last nerve. I started driving up the street. It seemed like the more I drove the louder she got. I couldn't take it anymore! I started screaming at her, "Be quiet!" At this point I guess he knew I was about to lose it. He said, "Pull the car over!" He got out, took her out of the car seat, and began to walk her up and down the street. He was singing to her and bouncing her, trying to calm her down. I just sat in the car wanting it all to go away.

Being high and having a crisis just don't mix! And I thank God today that someone came and got the baby, because I don't know what would have happened had he not come, because I was really high! He walked with Grace for hours before she finally stopped crying. We believed she had a contact high.

After he got her to stop crying, we drove around a little while. The baby went to sleep and we went back to my apartment. Ruben left, and the baby and I went to sleep. It wasn't long after that day that I realized I couldn't take care of this baby anymore. Also by this time my family realized that I had started smoking again and they told me to take the baby over to mom's house and leave her there. That was good for me! By doing so it allowed me to get buck wild again, but at least the baby was safe. I knew that Grace was going to be taken care of.

Now my husband, who said he wasn't going to pick Grace up, was helping my mother take care of her. Remember, my mother was running the laundromat and she had to take the baby to work with her everyday. Mom was now taking care of both my children and my husband was always around helping her and spending time with his son. My mom, being the wonderful woman she was, would put him to work, even if it meant him helping her take care of Grace. I believe that in doing so, he fell in love with her. The precious little girl that he said he would never pick up, never touch; he was now feeding, changing her diaper, rocking, holding, and putting to sleep. He was caring for Grace like she was his own.

Sybil's House

This time when I went back to the drugs, things for me became a little worse. It wasn't long after taking Grace to my mother's I was out on the street trying to make some money selling my body. Now don't get me wrong, I had done it before and that is how I became pregnant with Grace, but now I was taking it to the streets for real. I didn't want to be a prostitute so I would wait at the bus stop or walk away from my house and then walk back. When a man would pull up and ask me if I needed a ride I would tell them I was going home and agreed to take the ride. If they took me home or up the street away from my house, I would just get out, but if they propositioned me and I liked the deal, I would accept. I would do the deed, get the money and go and get high. This way in my mind it didn't seem like I was a prostitute, but of course, I was in denial.

One night I was standing at a bus stop and this guy stopped. He was driving a little sports car. He asked me if I needed a ride and I told him yes. I got in the car and he sped off. He immediately started to proposition me and I was asking questions. He then turned this corner and pulled over to the curb. I thought he wanted to stop and talk. While he was talking, he reached into his jacked pocket and quickly pulled out a handgun and pointed it at my head. Terrified for my life, I quickly tried to open the car door, but it hit the curb. I thought I was a dead woman. I didn't think I was going to be able to get out. It wasn't enough room. It was only a little space. I guess, because of the will to survive, I squeezed out of that tiny space like a mouse through a crack in a wall. I ran for my life down the street never looking back.

That night, he was the last person I tried to pick up. I knew it was dangerous in the streets, but when you are an addict your better judgment is over ruled. You do what you have to do to feed your addiction. And, you do what you don't want to do to feed it also!

One night I was out trying to be slick and sell my body again. I got in the car with a man, we made the deal, and he pulled over to the curb. I was wondering why he was acting suspicious. Then I heard those words, "You are under arrest!" I jumped out of the car only to run into a female cop. I tried to get away but she grabbed me. I didn't want to go to jail. It would be like having the brakes put on your life. I kept yanking, and pulling, trying to get away from this lady. In a very soft tone, she said, "Stop, just stop. You can't get away, stop!" It was something about the way she spoke to me. I looked at her, and then let her put the handcuffs on me. She put me in the back of the police car.

On the way to the police station the female cop started talking to me. She said, "Are you new at this?" I told her, "Yes!" She began to tell me how dangerous it was for me to be out in the streets doing what I was doing. I knew it was dangerous, but it was a chance I was forced to take by the addiction.

They took me to jail and booked me. I just knew my life was over. I didn't want to do jail time. I had never been in jail for an extended period of time. My mother had already warned me that if I went to jail, they were not going to bail me out. She had told me this ever since I was a child. I believe she used it as a precautionary measure. I really don't think she thought it would ever happen.

They put me in a cell with a lot of other woman. I must admit I was afraid. These women were in there for all sorts of reasons. I was scared but I couldn't let my fear be known. I knew I was a praying sister! Nobody knew that I was praying, but I was praying like never before. "Oh God, please help me and keep me safe." I met a few ladies who told me they wouldn't let anything happen to me. I believed them!

One night two girls were brought into our cell at the same time. I believe they were friends. Out of all the women in the cell, for some reason, they didn't like me! They told the other woman they were going to jump on me. I didn't take too kindly to the threat. I couldn't take on both of them. I knew I had to come up with something to protect myself.

When we had to line up for dinner, the guard yelled at me, "Go to the back of the line." I was very upset. I felt as if I was being picked on for no reason, and the girls that were bothering me were getting away with it. When everyone started walking to dinner she told me, "I did that on purpose because I wanted the girls to go on so I could put some space between you guys." I told her, "Thank You!" But when we got inside the dining area and I walked past their table, they started threatening me again. Some of the girls just looked and said, "Don't worry! We got your back!" I told myself, "Yea right." I didn't believe that anyone was going to take up for me.

I had to hear those girls' mouth the whole time we were at dinner. Of course I was very afraid and upset. All I could think about was some of the movies I had seen on television, and the horrible things that happened to women while they were in jail. I told myself, "I'm not going to be the one of those ladies." So fear set in big time!

I made something that I was going to use to defend myself (I won't tell because I don't want anyone to do what I did). If they decided to come after me while I was asleep I was going to let them have it. I remembered lying down on my bunk and basically praying myself to sleep. My plans were to stay awake, and I had everything in place. I woke up realizing I had fallen asleep. I was still holding my secret. Finally morning came and I was told they were released during the night. I was so relieved! One of the girls had some strange features. She looked like a horse by the mouth. They just came and left. They almost didn't look human! To be women they were really big and tall and mean looking. I don't know where they came from, and I don't know where they went, but I was glad that they were gone out of my life. It was the strangest thing!

After that episode the rest of the time in the jail wasn't that bad. I found a lot of women that liked reading the Bible and talking about the Lord. In our past time we would play cards and I would talk about my sweet Jesus. I know it was the Lord that was with me during that time because he knew jail wasn't the place for me. This time in jail I had to stay about twenty days. Those twenty days seemed like forever to me. You never knew what day was going to be your last.

I would have a scheduled court date, but when I went to court, I wouldn't get to see the judge. This happened several times. I was beginning to wonder what was going on? Finally one day they came and got me and told me I needed to get my things because I was going home. I was running around trying to say goodbye to the ladies. The officer yelled, "You better come on if you want to leave!" I left and I never went back.

My sister came and picked me up. It seem like the longest drive back to her house. I was hardly talking at all. I just wanted to look at the trees and the people going to and fro. Why I stared at the trees so much I don't know, but I glared at almost every tree until we reached her house. It was a real joy to see the cars and people in motion again. I was so elated to have my freedom back!

When we arrived at my sister's house, everyone was glad to see me of course. I was glad to see everyone, especially my children and I was glad to see my mom and dad. My dad never really said too much so I didn't know if he was glad to see me or not. Every now and then throughout the day, he would just look at me. That would leave me wondering!

I did well for a while staying clean and sober, but it didn't take long and I was off to the races again. I didn't use drugs for twenty days, so everyone including myself, thought that I was capable of staying drug free. I soon found out that the demons were still there. They were lying low waiting until I got out of jail. I thought they were gone for good! Once again, I thought that my days of drug addiction were over.

Being on the streets this time, I had to be really careful. If I got arrested again, I would be facing more jail time. I knew I didn't want to do that!

While I was incarcerated, I was evicted from my apartment. I lost everything that my family didn't get. I was furious! But, what could I really say? I knew people were getting tired of my mess and me. Of course, I was upset with everyone because I felt they could have done something to keep my stuff. In reality though, I probably would have smoked it up anyway! All of my memories were gone! I had a hard time dealing with that!

I went to the apartment and the door had a pad lock on it. I took my fist and punched the glass out. I opened the door and went in. Even though they told me I was evicted I went over there anyway. What in the world was I thinking? I wanted to get in, smoke my cocaine, and see if anything was left I guess. After I finishing freebasing, I figured I better leave, before someone noticed I had broken in and called the police.

I left and got on the City bus going to my mother's house. I sat there in a daze. I couldn't stop thinking, "All of my stuff is gone!" Mom said while I was in jail they had nowhere to put it, so they let the landlord have it. Suddenly I felt a tap on my shoulder. "Your hand is bleeding!" someone said to me. I was so upset and out of it, I didn't know I was bleeding. When I looked down at my hand, blood was everywhere. I just sat there and let it bleed!

I could feel eyes staring at me. I thought, "If I want to sit here and bleed to death then that is my business and not yours, just leave me alone." So I just sat there until I reached my stop. I had to walk a couple of blocks before I got to my mom's house. I found something to wipe the blood off my hand. I didn't want to hear her mouth when I got there. I still, to this day, have the scare on the top of my left hand.

Chapter 9 Recovery House

I realized I needed help but I couldn't make myself get the help I so desperately needed. While everyone was taking care of my children, I was out taking care of my needs, getting high. Now I had to deal with the fact that I had two children I wasn't taking care of, and that was heart breaking for me. As much as I wanted to do the right thing I couldn't. My family was really concerned about me and wanted me to get some help quickly.

My sister's boyfriend's brother knew of a recovery house where I could go get some help. It was around September of 1985 I checked into His Sheltering Arms which at the time was located on Avalon in Los Angeles CA. Now the facility has grown tremendously and is located on 11101 South Main Street. Mrs. Jeffries is the founder and president and now one of her daughters is the director. Ms. Jeffries is a little lady with a sweet spirit and a big heart. The program was well structured, and I had no problem fitting in.

At first, I didn't want to be there, but it didn't take me long to realize this was the best thing for me. I decided I would give it a try and work the program. We had to do a lot of writing and soul searching. I was willing to do it, but I must admit it was difficult. I still have some of the writings I did when I first starting the program. I met a lot of beautiful woman who were just like me. We all had problems with drugs and we wanted a solution.

Everyday we had to clean, cook, exercise, go to the doctor and have meetings. For the most part we all got along very well. We could go to church on Sunday if we desired. The church they took us to happened to be the same church my sister's boyfriend and brother attended. So I would have my sister come and bring my children so I could see them and hold them. While you are in the six-month program in the beginning stages (I believe it was the first 30 days) you were not allowed to have any contact with anyone outside of the house.

Everything was going well until I found out my high school was having our class reunion. I asked Ms. Jeffries if I could attend and she told me no. I couldn't understand why. I asked her if I could go to my mother's house after church and She said, "Yes, just make sure you get back to the house on time." I told her, "Okay." I went to my mother's house and my friend came. I figured it would be okay to run to the park for just a minute to the Dorsey class reunion. I had such a good time walking around seeing my old classmates, the time got away from me.

It felt good not to do any drugs or drink any alcohol like everyone else. For some reason, when you get a few days of sobriety, you really feel like you've accomplished something. I stayed sober but I stayed too long. When I returned to my mom's house, I had gotten a call from His Sheltering Arms and I wasn't there. When I talked to Mrs. Jeffries she asked me some questions. I lied of course. She told me I needed to come to the home and pick up my things. I was being put out of the program. I tried to talk her into letting me stay but to no avail. She refused to bend the rules for me. I couldn't understand?

If she really wanted to help me, and I was doing so well in the house, why couldn't I be given another chance? After all it wasn't like I had used any drugs while away. It seemed like such a long ride back to the recovery house. I was so ashamed; I didn't want to show my face. I had to immediately pack up my things and leave. It was sad hugging the ladies and telling them goodbye. I wasn't angry with Mrs. Jeffries because I knew that she was only doing her job. I was disappointed because I couldn't have a second chance but the rules were the rules!

My soon to be brother-in-law, Pastor Ron Wright, called me at my mom's house to encourage me to seek another recovery house. He felt I really needed to finish the program. I had already completed over thirty days. I figured if I continue to work the 12-step program, go to church, I would be fine and I wouldn't need to go to another recovery house. I did what I needed to do. I prayed, read my Bible and I went to church. I was doing really well, so I thought! I was even witnessing to others and telling them about the Lord. Days had passed and others thought I was clean and sober once and for all!

Relapse

One day my girlfriend who lived up the street called. I turned her on to drugs and she was still using. I immediately started talking to her about the Lord. I told her she needed to get some help like I did and get off of the drugs once and for all. She said, "Can you take a ride with me?" I told her, "Yes!" I thought I would use this time to finish witnessing to her. The whole time we were driving I was talking. I couldn't believe she went and bought some cocaine. We went back to her house. I was still talking to her about drugs and the Lord.

Instead of me telling her to drop me off at my mom's house, I went with her to her house. When she parked I could have walked home because mom's house was up the street. I talked to her about drugs until she was finished cooking the cocaine. She took a hit off the pipe, handed it to me and I took a hit too. All the counseling and witnessing had come to a halt. I was off to the races again. I couldn't stop smoking, I just couldn't! I stayed out for days using before I went back to my mother's house.

I was back using! I was too embarrassed to go home because everyone thought I was going to be all right this time. Everyone, except my soon to be brother-in-law, Pastor Ron Wright. He told me I needed more help, and I told him I was good. I was not good!

One thing I noticed, every time I stopped using drugs, and went back, I got worse. I would venture out a little further. I was getting pretty bad off and began using for longer periods of time. I would smoke for four to seven days at a time.

During that time I would consume little or no food. Every time I got really hungry, all I had to do was hit a cigarette or smoke some Cocaine and the hunger pains would go away. I was really beginning to lose too much weight. I really looked bad. I couldn't see it though!

Skeleton

One day when I went to my mother's house and Sharmel was in the kitchen, I looked in the mirror and I screamed. She came running in the bathroom and said, "Sha what is wrong with you?" I said, "Look at my face!" "Look at my eyes!" She said, "I know, that's what we've been trying to tell you, you look sick!" But until that moment I couldn't see it.

I was so thin you could see the sockets that housed my eyeballs. When I looked at myself in the mirror I literally scared myself. I looked like a monster. My mom said I had the look of death because I was so black.

One day when I still had my apartment, I had eaten all of the food except for rice and butter. I was hungry so I decided to boil the rice and add butter. When the rice was gone, I was hungry again. I remember sticking my finger in the butter and eating it. I was famished! I told myself, " I can not just eat butter!" So I called a friend of the family who owned a little restaurant on the corner of Adams and Houser called "Erma's". I asked her if I could have something to eat, and when I got some money I would pay her back. She told me sure to come on down and get something to eat. I was so embarrassed, but hunger overrides shame.

When I arrived she treated me like I was a paying customer. She fixed me a hamburger and fries. I remember going to the window that looked out onto Adams Boulevard. I wanted to sit there and watch the cars go by. I took one bite of the hamburger. I thought I was going to have a heart attack. My heart began to race uncontrollably! I guess I was so hungry my body didn't know how to respond to the food. I thought I had better wait a minute before I took another bite because I didn't want to bust my heart. And, I must admit the food was very good.

Am I Dying?

A friend wanted me to cook all of his cocaine one day. I gladly said, "Okay." I didn't have to go far. He was going to have me do it at a friend of ours who lived directly across the street from my mom. He had a whole lot of it, so I knew I was going to have a good time. These were the type of people I liked to help out. While I was cooking, of course I had to test each rock to make sure it was perfect. He was very generous, so we were smoking it as fast as I was cooking it. All of a sudden something strange began to happen to me. I didn't want to stop cooking, but I was beginning to feel faint. It was a really weird feeling that I had never felt before. I didn't know what was going on with me but I knew it was serious. For me to stop smoking, with all of that free cocaine around, I knew something serious was going on.

Suddenly, I just stopped cooking and headed for the front door. They asked me where was I going and I just kept on walking. "I have to go" I said (and probably said some other stuff that I don't remember). I had to walk up this long driveway just to make it to the street. As I was crossing the street, I stopped right in the middle. I froze in my tracks. I remember my mother saying, "Sha get out of the street!" I could hear her, but I couldn't move. All I could do was stand there! Finally somebody came and got me out of the street and they rushed me to the emergency room.

The doctor's didn't know what was wrong with me. An IV was started right away. I was severely dehydrated and malnourished. They couldn't get a pulse on my hand so they went down to my ankles to try and get a pulse. The doctor's were afraid they were going to loose me. I remember seeing my mom fall back against the wall. They ran a lot of test to see what was going on with me. That's all I remember them telling me that was wrong. There were many days I deliberately put myself in harms way, hoping someone would take my life. Now that I was actually at deaths door I realized I didn't want to die.

I stayed there for a few days before I was finally able to go home. I had to be on bed rest. I was very, very weak. I lay in bed like an infant, sleeping and eating until I got my strength back. Mom of course waited on me hand and foot.When I got my strength back, I was off to the drugs again. By this time, mom was really getting tired of the drugs and me. She was praying and trying everything she could think of to help her poor child. My mom was really trying to get me out of California to get some help. I too, would cry out to God saying, "If you get me out of California, I know I can stay saved Lord."

During my madness, my husband had become homeless himself. When he reached rock bottom he decided to join the military with his friend. He ended up getting stationed in Kentucky. My mom arranged for me to go and visit him for a week. She wanted so much for me to get my life together. I really didn't want to go, but because he bought the ticket I went.

In June of 1986, I was off to KY to visit for a week. I was so excited now. My mom said, "Oh Michael must really be something in the Army, he said the Limousine was going to come and pick you up." "A Limousine!" I said, "What is he doing in the Army that he could have a Limousine come and get me from the airport?" I was reluctant because I had never been on a plane before. We had always traveled by car or bus. To fly for the first time by myself was a challenge for me. I can't believe it, but I went. I really didn't have a relationship with my husband. But I was curious to see what was going on!

The take off was the scariest part of the whole trip to me. I remember quietly screaming, and clenching the armrest. I couldn't believe I was actually flying by myself. The whole time I was on the plane I wondered what it was my husband did in the military. Before I knew it the flight was over. It was really not bad. When I got to Nashville, Tennessee. I was excited. I was looking for my husband and this big Limousine waiting to pick me up. He must really be somebody to be picking me up in a Limo! To my surprise, the Limousine was actually a fifteen passenger Van. We had to ride over an hour in this crowded van to Fort Campbell, Kentucky.

Our airport in Los Angeles was only about fifteen minutes away. I was very disappointed and I asked myself the whole ride, "What have I gotten myself into?" Finally we arrived to the base and we stayed in a guest room, which is like a mini hotel.

It was located on the military instillation. I said to myself, "Okay." It wasn't what I had imagined, but it wasn't bad either. The nerve of a crack head huh!

Our stay together was as if we had never parted. We would do well until he began to ask me questions. I didn't want to talk about my past or my street life. He had to go to work everyday. But, that was okay with me, because all I did was eat, sleep, and watch television. These were things I didn't get to do on a regular basis. I would get up and get dressed when I knew he was coming back from work. Mommy had taken me shopping, so I had all new clothes. She wanted me to look my best. When he got off duty, we would do something everyday.

Michael and I went for walks, museum, and movies. On the weekend we even went to a club. For some reason I didn't enjoy myself in the club which I thought was strange, because I used to love to party and dance. I remember he wanted to dance with someone else and he asked me if it was okay. I told him to go on. You would have thought that I told him to go and dance all night long with someone else. He left me alone for the longest time. I couldn't believe it. At first I began to wonder if something had happened to him. Guys were asking me to dance, but I was so pissed, all I wanted to do was leave. If I had not been in a foreign land I would have. That wasn't a good night for us. I vowed I would never go to a club with him again. Finally he decided to show up with a big grin on his face.

Immediately he asked me what was wrong. I used a few choice words to express what was wrong with me. With this big grin on his face he said, "You told me to go and have a good time!" I told him, "That's a lie, I told you to go dance, not stay gone all night!"

By now, he knew that I was pissed, and it was time to go. I asked myself, "How in the world could you do that to someone? He knew that I didn't know anybody there. Maybe he thought I would fit in like I do in Los Angeles." I actually felt like I had been abandoned, and stranded. It wasn't a good feeling at all.

Unfortunately, I didn't enjoy myself at all. I believe he enjoyed himself. I vowed I wouldn't ever let that happen to me again. Of course he did apologize to me, but that didn't change the fact I was upset about the entire evening. I really couldn't express to him how it made me feel. Besides he had been drinking, and I knew that it would be pointless to try. So we just went to bed. As I lay there, I tried to forget what had just happened to me but it kept replaying the whole night in my mind, until I fell asleep.

As the morning was dawning I was awaken by my husband. It took me a while to get myself together. I had to come out of the dream I was in, figure out where I was, and what was I doing there. My husband being the man that he is was jolly like nothing had happened the night before. So I just played it off too, like nothing ever happened. After all, in just a few days I would be leaving this place, going back home. I must admit though, I did have a good night sleep.

Sleep, sleep, wonderful sleep! I really enjoyed sleeping because I would be able to escape from reality. All of my hurts and pain would seem to go away when I was asleep. When I would wake up, I would feel great for a few seconds. Then I would be reminded of what was really going on in my life. The sadness would set right back in. Sometimes I really couldn't believe I was living the way I was. There were days it was so bad, I had to pinch myself to figure out if I was awake or sleep. I know now I was getting real close to insanity! Sometimes I really didn't know!!!!! So this particular night I enjoyed my sleep.

Day after day he kept asking me, "What do you want to do?" and I would tell him, "What ever you want to do!" I really didn't have anything in particular I wanted to do. I wasn't like your typical tourist. Then he asked me, "Do you want to go and get some dope or something? To my amazement I said, "No" and I meant it! I really didn't have any cravings for cocaine, at all. Not for the entire seven days I was there. I guess I wasn't any fun to him, but what he failed to realize, I was enjoying this nice clean environment. I was content, eating, resting and watching television. One day after work he decided to take me to a pawnshop to buy me a ring. Both of us admired the same ring called a "Tigers Eye".

Michael purchased it and placed it on my finger. I was really surprised and gave him a big hug and kiss. It was a very unique ring and I loved looking at it on my finger.

I was all packed and ready to go back home. My seven-day vacation was over. It was really good seeing Michael doing well in the Military. He was finally making something out of his life and I was proud of him. I must say I was a bit concerned about his drinking though! On the way to the airport, we engaged in really good conversation. We said our goodbyes and I was off with no strings attached. Yes we were still married, but he was there in Kentucky doing his thing (I wasn't stupid), and I was going back to California to do my thing. We didn't ask each other any questions. So kiss, kiss goodbye!

When I arrived back in Los Angeles, I couldn't wait to see my children. Everyone was excited to see each other and it felt good to be back on familiar territory. Of course mom had a lot of questions to ask. She wanted to know all about my trip. The limousine threw her off too! I really got a laugh telling her about the fifteen-passenger van. I guess when you live in California and you say limo, we associate it with a stretch limousine.

I shared with momma that Michael had to work every day and I got plenty of rest. I showed her the ring and she smiled. I knew she was up to something, but I was simply going through the motions.

To me it was just a vacation. It was an experience, and it was over.

It was strange how I felt the entire time I was in Kentucky. I don't know what happened to me while I was there, but I wasn't Sha, the drug addict. I wasn't the person that had just left Los Angeles. I had no desire for drugs and drank a small amount of alcohol and smoked my cigarettes. After mom heard everything I had to say about the trip, I think she thought I had kicked the habit for good. All the while, I could feel the urge coming on. I let her believe it though. I decided to take Grace and Michael to the park. While the children were playing and having a good time, I was trying to figure out what lie I was going to tell to get out of the house later that evening. I was ready to find some cocaine and get high. I didn't have to spend any of the money I took to Kentucky and Michael gave me a few dollars when I left. I was straight!

I figured out a plan. I was going to pretend I wanted to go visit some friends. I enjoyed the children until I couldn't resist the urge. The thoughts were becoming too intense. Besides, it was starting to get dark and we had to walk back to the house.

I remember going in and telling mom what a good time we had at the park. I tried to sit around for a minute or two but I had to go. When my mother went towards the back of the house I shouted, "I'll be right back I'm going to see my friend around the corner for a minute." I quickly went out the front door, locked it and left. I started walking briskly up the street. I didn't look back. I was listening though, because I thought she was going to call for me to come back. "Hurry, hurry," I kept telling myself. Hurry and get to the corner before she calls your name. I couldn't run because I didn't want to make it seem like I was trying to get away. Finally, I made it to the corner and across Labrea to my friend's house. I was hoping he was at home and had something to smoke or knew where to get some.

I liked going to his house because he seemed to be honest and he never made a pass at me. As I arrived to the house, I paused and took a look around. I had been gone a week and I wanted to make sure he still lived there. I didn't want to walk into the back of his house and be surprised.

I knocked on the door and he (let's call him Bob) swung the door open as if he was surprised and happy to see me. Bob was a disabled addict, but he was such a gentleman. He was actually a father and a husband when I met him. Soon after he lost his job, his wife, and then his home. He was staying in a tiny room. It was a 10'x5' space behind the house he once lived in. He had enough room for a twin bed, TV and a few other things.

Bob would go to the library to clean himself up because he didn't have a bathroom or kitchen. He didn't own a car either. Sometimes the little hole in the walls was the best place to get high!

Bob and I were cool smoking buddies. Lucky for me, Bob was able to score. Sadly for me, one hit sent me off to the races. I thought because I had not smoked in a week I would be able to stay in control. I took that rock and placed it on the pipe, lit my torch and placed it on top of the rock. Pulling slow and gentle I inhaled and held it until I couldn't hold it no more. Slowly I began to blow it out. It was as if I had lit the pilot of my soul. It's an indescribable feeling that will send you on a chase for more and more. I began chasing that rock like never before.

I stayed gone until I spent all my money. I even took the ring my husband had just bought me and pawned it to some guy for cocaine. Some time later when I went back to get it, he said he didn't have it. I was angry, but what could I do about it? Nothing! After staying in the street a few days, I decided to go home. Everyone was upset with me, especially my mother. I know she thought the vacation she and my husband put together had made a change in my life. She was sure I was healed! That couldn't be further from the truth. The week vacation seemed to have made things worse than before because I was off to the races again.

Things had gotten pretty bad between Ruben and me. He couldn't stand me because I wouldn't listen to him. How could I control myself for him, when I couldn't control myself for myself, my children, my parents or anyone else? That was the hardest thing for him to understand. He would get so mad at me.

One day he threatened to pour acid on my face and disfigure me. He said when he finished no one was going to want to have anything to do with me because I was going to be too ugly to look at. That really scared me because I knew what he had done to me in the past. He was becoming more and more hostile as the days went by. I always managed to trigger something to set him off. When he threatened me I believed him. Whenever I went out to get high, I always had to look over my shoulder. He had a way of always showing up and making my life a living hell.

I can't remember all of the things that he did to me, but I can tell you he always told me that he loved me. He did help me by giving me some information about section 8 housing and I was able to get an apartment. In the beginning of the relationship when he tried to leave me, I should have let him go.

I believe he started changing when I gave him a hit off of the pipe! I tell you that stuff will make a monster out of some people. When we began to smoke together it was bad. He couldn't stand for me to smoke anywhere without him and I didn't always want to smoke with him. If I wanted to smoke and he wasn't around I did it. In his eyes that wasn't right. I remember one day he told me I could take him to work and keep his truck. "Just be there on time to pick me up!" he said. I decided to smoke that night and I couldn't make myself stop and go pick him up. I was sitting in a parking lot in the back of the van. I was smoking and watching the clock trying to figure out what I was going to tell him. It was getting later and later while I kept smoking trying to get the story straight. I didn't stop to go get him until I was completely out of cocaine. Then, I finally went and picked him up.

When I made it to his job, it was dark and all the cars were gone from entire parking lot. I found him walking around aimlessly. I pulled up beside him, put the truck in park, got out of the van and walked to the passenger side. With a smile on his face, he put his arms around me and gave me a kiss. When we started driving out the parking lot he gently asked me, "Where you been honey?" I began trying to explain. He immediately got upset. He pulled the van over on the shoulder of the freeway. He started yelling, "Get out of the van!" I did. I could feel my heart begin to race as I stood on the shoulder waiting for him to make his way to me. As the cars are racing past us, and the light shinning on him, I could see a gun in his hand. Before I knew it, he grabbed me and tried to throw me off the side of the freeway. I grabbed him and we both almost fell off the side. It was a long drop to the bottom. He pushed me and said, "You better run bitch." My first thought was to run like he told me to, but I didn't want to die of a gunshot wound in the back of the head! I told him, "No I'm not gonna run! If you want to shot me, you're gonna have to shot me in the face!"

He snatched me around and threw me into the front seat of the van. He got in the van and sped off. Yelling at the top of his lungs he repeatedly kept asking me, "Where you been Sha? Huh? Where you been? Why do you keep doing this to me? Why? Answer me!" Crying, I told him, "I don't know! I don't know! I'm sorry, I'm sorry I couldn't stop smoking!" He said, "Who you been smoking with Sha, Who you been with?" I told him, "Nobody, I was smoking by myself!" He said, "All this time Sha? You expect me to believe that, huh?" I could tell by the sound of his voice he was really upset this time. His voice sounded like he was crying and I could see the spit flying out of his mouth as he was yelling at me. No matter what I said, he didn't believe me.

Suddenly, he snatched me by my hair. I literally heard the hair in the top of my head come out of my hair follicles. I could see a wad of my hair in the palm of his hand. I couldn't believe he had just pulled my hair out. At this point I was petrified and in a lot of pain. My head felt like I had just lost part of my scalp. He was so angry I thought he was going to kill me.

Ruben lived out in the valley and nobody knew where he lived. I didn't want to go to his house but I couldn't get out of the van. When we got there I was in excruciating pain. He took me into his place and had his way with me. As he was doing his thing to me, he told me, "You know I love you and I only do this for your own good." Like a dummy, I believed every word he said. When he was done, I lay there on the couch and I cried myself to sleep. After all, I was just a bad girl!

Another time I was at a house where Ruben was banned. I was smoking and didn't know he was waiting for me outside. As I was leaving, he pulled up from out of nowhere and said, "Get in Sha!" We were sitting there talking, or shall I say he was interrogating me. I wasn't giving him the answers he wanted to hear, so he pulled out his pocketknife and pointed it at me. I just sat there and continued to give him the right answers. All of a sudden he took the knife and put it in my side. I felt a little stick, but I didn't move. He just kept the knife there and I just kept sitting there. Finally, I got out of the van and I told him I was going home. I was right up the street from my mother's house. I went in and went to bed.

I had to go to school the next morning. When I didn't get up, my mother came into the room just like she used to when I was in high school. She walked past the room a couple of times yelling, "Sha get up, you're going to be late for school." When I didn't get up, she came in the room and yelled, " Get up" and she pulled the covers back. When she pulled the covers back she screamed, "What happened to you?" I told her, "Nothing happened to me!" She said, "Why are you bleeding then?" I was so high I didn't feel the knife when it broke my skin. Ruben had actually pierced me in the side and blood had been oozing out of me all night onto the sheets. I was lying there in a pool of blood. It scared my mother so bad. She was furious! She said, "Call and tell him he better come and take you to the hospital." I did, and he came and took me to the hospital.

Ruben coached me as to what to say when we got there. He said, "If you tell them the truth, they are going to take me away, and you will not see me for a while." I just looked at him as if we both were crazy "Tell them you fell off the back of my motorcycle," he said. I just looked at him. When the doctor's came into the room, the first thing one of them asked me was, "How did this happen?" "I fell off the back of a motorcycle," I said. They gave us a look of disbelief, but they stitched me up and let me go. I still have the scare on my side.

Once when I was out around town smoking and he was looking for me. Everywhere I went, someone told me a man had come by looking for me. I would always ask what he looked like and they would describe Ruben. One night I made my way over to the Labrea Hotel to get high with some friends. A couple of people left, he questioned them, and they told him where I was. He came banging on the door. I asked one of the guys not to open the door, but he said he was leaving because he didn't want any trouble. I asked him to tell Ruben I wasn't there. I went into the bathroom and hid inside the cabinet under the double sink. When the guy opened the door to leave I could hear them talking. Ruben said,

"Hey man isn't there a young lady in here with you?" The guy said, "Naw man, I don't know what you're talking about" Ruben said, "Some people just left here and they told me she was in there man!" He told him again, "Man, I don't know what you're talking about." He closed the door and walked away.

I decided I better stay under the sink for a minute to make sure the coast was clear. I knew how Ruben was and he didn't give up easy. Just when I thought it was safe to come out, I heard the door to the room open. I could hear two men talking. It was Ruben and the hotel manager. He talked him into letting him in the room. As they were looking around, the manager kept telling him, "There's no one in this room." Ruben kept insisting I was in there. He said, "I know I didn't see her come out!" I could hear his voice getting closer and closer to the bathroom. As he was looking around he opened the cabinet door.

Immediately, I climbed out from up under the cabinet. They both looked on in amazement. As Ruben was smiling telling the manager, "See man, I knew she was in here!" I took off running. He didn't expect me to run. I wasn't going to get beat that night. I ran like lightning. I ran out of the hotel parking lot, across six lanes of traffic on Labrea to mom's house about two and a half blocks away. I ran up on the porch so fast I thought I was going to slam into the front door. I banged, and banged on the front door until my mother answered. She asked me, "What's wrong?" I told her I had to get away from Ruben so I ran home. Momma said, "Oh Lord Sha!"

Time and time again I had to sustain some sort of abuse from Ruben because he wanted to tame me and I was untamable. I wasn't only going to do what I wanted to do, but I was going to do what the drugs were telling me to do. I WAS TOTALLY OUT OF CONTROL! It didn't matter how many times I was beaten. If you didn't kill me, I wasn't going to stop! I knew the only way to stop was to get DELIVERED from the drugs or DIE! Those were the only two ways!!

Ruben was always looking for me. He was on a constant manhunt. One time I was in a very large house freebasing, filled with people smoking everywhere. I was standing in front of a wall and I heard a voice in my head say, "Leave." I had not finished what I had so I just stood there and took another hit. Again, I heard a voice say, "Leave." I wasn't ready to leave. I had plenty of cocaine left to smoke and I was enjoying myself. No one was bothering me and it was cool. I heard the voice in my head this time say, "Leave, LEAVE NOW!" I began to gather my things quickly. People started asking me, "What's the matter? Where are you going?" I said, "I'll be back" and I made my way to the door and I left swiftly. I started walking briskly away from that house. I kept walking until I found a quiet place to stop and take another hit.

I smoked all night here and there. Early the next morning, I decided to go back to the house where I was the night before. When the owner let me in, he asked me, "Did you hear what happened here last night?" I said, "No, what? He said, "This man came by here looking for a girl named Sha, we told him there was no one here by that name." He said, "Okay and he left." He said, "The next thing we knew, we heard gunshots everywhere. He had come back and was shooting up the place!" I said, "What!" Then he walked me over to the wall and showed me the bullet holes. One of them was right where I had been standing all night getting high.

Had I not listened to the voice, I would have gotten shot in the head. All I could do was look on in awe. I didn't use the name "Sha" when I was in the streets. I used a different name because I didn't want people to know that I was my mother's daughter. If someone were talking to my mother about what was going on in the streets, she wouldn't hear my name. I didn't want to embarrass her like that. I later found out she was having people look for me. That's why they couldn't find me! WHY DID THAT VOICE WARN ME THAT NIGHT?

I would put myself in harms way because I couldn't stop myself and I was too afraid to take my own life. There were many times I came close to death. When Ruben said he was going to pour acid on my face, I believed him. I knew what he was capable of doing. I was scared, but not too scared to stop. I kept looking over my shoulder and smoking cocaine. I finally realized he really didn't love me like he kept telling me he did.

All I wanted to do was get high in peace. I didn't want all the drama and violence that came with it. After the acid threat from Ruben, I told myself I couldn't keep going on like this. I knew I had to leave him alone. I had to stop running from the enemy. I made a conscious decision to leave him. From that day on when Ruben called my mother's house, I wouldn't say a word; I would hang up the phone. He would wait a few days and call back again. I would hang up at the sound of his voice. One day he called and yelled, "Sha, don't hang up baby. Please just listen to me for a minute. I have something to tell you." For some reason, that day I didn't hang up and I listened. He said, "I'm going to the mountains to get some help. I've met these people, and they're going to help me get off these drugs. You won't be able to get a hold of me, so I just wanted to let you know where I was going." He also said, "You should try and get yourself some help too." I didn't say a word. When I felt he was done talking, I hung up the phone and I didn't talk to him again for many, many, years.

I was glad he was going to get some help, but at the same time, I didn't know for sure. When I went out, I was still looking over my shoulders for him because I knew how he was.

Chapter 11: All Alone

With Ruben out of my life, I kept on using. I was really street walking now. I didn't know what I was doing, but I was out there trying to make it work. I didn't have anyone watching out for me and I didn't know where to go. I was getting worse and worse. It seemed as if all the dope addicts on the streets were worse too. It wasn't really any fun anymore. You could hardly trust anybody. I would go to a dope house, have someone score for me, and they would bring back very little or nothing at all and tell you all sorts of lies.

I remember one night I sent a girl to score for me. When she got back, she didn't have the cocaine or the money. She told me, "When I threw the money up, it didn't reach the window, and then I couldn't find it on the ground." I told her, "You better go find my money or bring the dope back." She left again and came back empty handed. I went to the place with her and it was true. We were at an apartment complex and they wanted us to throw the money up to the second floor window and the guy would drop down the dope. The money didn't have a chance of reaching up there. I told her, "If you don't get my money or my cocaine, I'm going to kill you and I'm not playing!" I was furious!

At that moment I realized I needed help. When I spoke those words, "Kill you," something inside of me went off. I was at my breaking point. I wasn't a violent person, and I couldn't believe I was talking about killing someone over some dope. That night when I got my cocaine, I didn't want to smoke with anyone.

I remembered walking home in the dark and I found a quiet place on the steps of my mother's back door. I sat down there, smoked, and cried. I cried, and I cried, and I cried! I cried out to God, and I asked him, "Please help me, I'm out of control!"

I had literally gone from the pent house to the gutter. I didn't like it, but I couldn't stop myself. I couldn't believe that I was talking about killing someone over drugs! I was getting so sick and tired of people using me, and talking to me any kind of way they pleased. I was called "crack head, dope phene and strawberry." They would laugh at you when you came in and when you left. They would say things like, "Look at her, she walked in like a trojan, and crawled out like a snail (when all of your money was gone). They would take your money and give you just a little piece of dope and tell you, "Bitch, you better get the hell out of here before I hurt you."

That really hurt my feelings and made me mad. I would sit and plot how I was going to get those people back for doing me wrong. But I wouldn't do anything. It wasn't in my heart to do such a thing. Not yet anyway! The night I told the girl I would kill her if she didn't get my money, I knew I was at my breaking point. I wasn't going to take too much more abuse. I wanted to hurt all of those who were hurting me. I knew I needed to get out of the game because that wasn't me. I didn't mind hurting myself, but I didn't like other people hurting me. I didn't want to hurt anyone! I had had enough. Just like all of the rapes, I felt like if I got raped one more time I was going to SNAP!

Raped, Raped, Raped!

I was raped so many times I decided to give it a chapter of its own. Being molested is a terrible thing for a little girl. After the molestations it seemed that from that point on, the sexual demons were after me, and they wouldn't leave me alone. I was young and didn't know what to do so I did nothing. I knew that if I told someone, all of the blame would point back at me. Each time it occurred, I prayed that it would never happen again. A relative was the culprit. I also fell victim to an old man who lived in the neighborhood. He molested me, and a lot of other young children. Afterwards, he would give me coins to go to the store. To this day, I don't know why I didn't tell somebody. I believe once that demonic door is open, things will continue to happen until it is closed!

Being raped is a horrific ordeal for a woman to have to endure. Being raped repeatedly is insane! One time I went to a motel with a guy I really didn't know. It wasn't uncommon for me to do so. We were at a house smoking together and he asked me if I wanted to go with me somewhere else to get high. I said yes and he got a room at the LaBrea Hotel. We immediately started smoking. After a few hits he wanted to get in bed. When I refused, he pushed me down on the bed and then he slapped me. At that point I was shocked and afraid. This had never happened to me because usually whomever I went with, we would just smoke and leave. I just laid there. When he was done I got myself together and left. I walked in the dark and cried, and cried! I was scared and angry. I didn't know this guy and I hadn't seen him around before. I couldn't understand why he did this to me. For some reason that night I didn't have any fight in me and I hated myself for that.

Another time I was sent to score for Ruben and myself. I was told that they had some good stuff at this apartment complex. Usually someone else would go for me but he wanted me to go this time. I knocked on this large, black, iron security door. No one came, so I banged on the door. A guy came to the door and asked, "What do you want?" I asked him, "Do you have anything?" He opened the door. I asked for a particular person and he said, "He is not here." I asked him, "Do you know when he is coming back?" Then he asked me, "What do you need?" When I told him I wanted to buy some cocaine, he immediately pulled out a gun and told me, "Get on the floor!" The house was dark with a glimmer of light coming from the kitchen area. I asked him, "What for?" He told me, "Get on the floor bitch, before I shoot you!" I got on the floor and he got down on top of me. I told him, "Please don't do this!" Loud and roughly he said, "Shut up!" So I just lay there on that nasty floor until he finished. Hoping and praying all the while that some one would come and make him stop. Where was Ruben when I needed him? When he finished, he had the audacity to talk about how good his non-consensual sex was to him, while he was heading to the bathroom. I was trying to get my clothes on so I could get out of there. Wet and all, I didn't care. If I could just get to the security door! I had almost reached the door, and he began yelling at me and calling me names. He said, "I ought to blow your Mother F…. brains out, you got all of this S… all over me! Why you didn't tell me you were on your period? Now I got all of this S… on me!" I told him, "I didn't know I was on my period!" He started calling me more names and told me to get out of his house. I took off running to the car. I was crying and I told Ruben who was waiting for me. He got his gun and we went back looking for the guy but we didn't find him anywhere.

For the most part, I didn't like for Ruben to take out his gun for any reason, but I do believe I would have stood there and let him shoot that guy. I didn't even know this guy and wasn't able to get a good look at him because it was so dark in the apartment. I went back to my apartment and cleaned myself up. I tried to escape from the PAIN, PAIN, PAIN, PAIN!

I was getting high at one of the spots that I used to frequent. A nice guy I knew from town was there and he asked me if I wanted to leave and go with him somewhere else to get high. We went to a hotel off of Labrea and Washington. Usually when I would run into him at a spot he would have plenty of dope, and we would get high until it was gone. Never anything sexual, so I felt safe with him. When we arrived at the room, strangely he knocked and someone opened the door. I thought he would have had a key.

A guy opened the door and we walked in. My friend closed the door and I was stunned. I didn't move any further. I asked myself, "What in the world is going on in this place?" I stood, looking slowly, scanning the small room and I couldn't believe what I was seeing. There were men everywhere! Some were walking around and some were sitting down.

Everyone was very quite. The atmosphere was very strange. It seemed as if they were up to something. The guy I came with politely said, "Have a seat." I asked myself, "If I leap for the door will I be able to make it out of here alive? If I scream will anybody hear me? Will they help me or will they even care? If they want to help me will they be able to help me in time? Oh my God, what in the world is going to happen to me tonight?" I sat at the foot of the bed near the door. There were two beds in the room. I know it must have been about fifteen guys in this small area. What were all of these guys doing in this room? And the big question was, what was I doing there with them? As I sat there watching the guy who brought me there, I kept asking myself, "What are they going to do to me?"

Some of them spoke and some didn't. No one was talking to me, but I could feel them looking, and I could hear them whispering. Unfortunately, I couldn't understand what they were saying to each other. I could sense something unpleasant was about to go down. The guy that I came with sat on a table right in front of me. He was moving slow. It reminded me of a Clint Eastwood movie, where nobody was talking and the camera was just showing the actors eyes. He placed a big rock on the pipe, hit it and then passed it to me smiling! I took the pipe and hit it passed it around. He always gave Big hits. On this night I felt he was giving me big hits for another reason. I was terrified for my life. I had never felt so helpless. I was trying to figure out what I should do because I wasn't in the mood for being "gang raped." I remember praying, "OH GOD PLEASE HELP ME! PLEASE, GOD, PLEASE DON'T LET THIS HAPPEN TO ME, PLEASE!" I remember staring at the guy as if my spirit was having a talk with his spirit. I looked at him with a plea in my eyes. Every now and then he would look at me as if to say, "It won't be that bad just take another hit." I kept staring at him and it's as if the big hits of cocaine were not doing me any good because my adrenalin was rushing. As I continued to stare at him pleading with my eyes, gently and softly out of the blue, my friend told me, "You can go!" I jumped up, he opened the door, and I took off running. I was so scared I went straight home and I was in for the night. I remember thanking my God for saving me that night.

I continued to get myself involved in one mess after another. I met a guy and he asked me to go with him to his place to get high. We drove for quite a while before we got there. I was in unfamiliar territory. When we arrived, he parked in a parking lot and we walked around a brick wall and ended up in a back yard. He told me his parents lived in the front house and he stayed in the garage in the back yard being used as a house. We smoked and smoked and then he wanted to have sex. I didn't want to and he told me I owed him. No one knew I was there. He made me get undressed and have sex with him and then he took my clothes. He said he was going to take them and have them washed. He put a lock on the door and I couldn't get out. I had been kidnapped. I didn't know what to do.

I figured if I played his game, sooner or later I would be able to break free. After a few days of this madness he was beginning to gain my trust. I made it seem like I enjoyed being there with him. Needless to say, that couldn't be further from the truth. To top it off, he didn't have any more cocaine. Finally, one day he let me take something to the trash can outside. I still didn't have my clothes back and was wearing his clothing. I took off running through the parking lot, never looking back. I saw a man and asked him if he would give me a ride back home. These events are still fresh in my mind after 20 years.

This is the last one I will share and it was the worst of them all. I had gone to a somewhat familiar place to score. I had only been there a few times. As I mentioned before, things on the street were beginning to change. People were changing and the game was changing too. It was rough. More and more people were selling and using drugs everywhere. This was a new spot I had found.

I went to the door and they told me to come on in. There were a lot of guys and girls in this house. I was told to go to the back room and get some cocaine from a particular person. I went into to the room; I scored, then I asked if I could smoke it there. He said,

"I don't care." When all of my drugs were gone he wanted me to perform a sexual act for some more. I didn't want to do it because I didn't know this guy. We sat there and got high with some of his stuff. He was the dope dealer, and I guess he felt he had given me enough. He then told me what I was going to do if I liked it or not. I told him, "No, I don't want to do it!" He pulled out his gun and began forcing my head down on his penis. As I kept pulling my head back, he continued to pull my head down and force his penis into my mouth. I kept pulling back and he kept forcing it until sometimes I would gag so bad I thought I was going to throw up. It crossed my mind to bite the thing off, but I knew I would probably get killed that day in that apartment. One part of me wanted to take the chance and another part of me didn't. This went on for what seemed like forever. He stopped when he realized I wasn't going to do it to him. He told me, "Get out!" I remember grabbing my face and rushing out of the apartment. People were looking at me as I ran down the stairs glancing back to make sure no one was coming after me.

As I began to walk down the street, I was crying like a baby. There was no one there this time to go and retaliate for me. It was broad daylight. People could see me as I walked down the street crying. I just wanted to die. I was so hurt. "Why, why?" I SCREAMED! "Why do people keep doing this to me, why?" I walked and walked and cried. People in their cars were looking at me as I crossed the street.

Nobody bothered to stop and help me. I walked all the way to my mother's house, which was about twelve blocks. When I got there I had to sit on the porch until somebody came home to let me in.

My mouth was hurting really bad. I went straight to the bathroom to wash my face and rinse out my mouth. It burned so bad and when I looked inside of my mouth to see what was going on. I couldn't believe what I was seeing! I thought the tears were blurring my vision. I wiped away the tears and looked again. "Oh my God, it's ripped off," I said. My tongue was literally ripped from the skin underneath it. The area that connects your tongue to the bottom of your mouth and keeps it from going down your throat is called the "frenulum linguae." Well it was completely ripped! My first thought was to go to the doctor, but then I faced the possibility of having to tell what happened to me. Will they believe me, and will they be able to do anything for me? I was so used to being blamed for everything until I didn't want to tell what had happened to me. I didn't tell a soul. My mouth was so sore for a long time. I didn't think my tongue would ever heal. It looked irreparable.

After an extended period of time, it finally did heal itself. Now it looks like it used to. Just writing about this is very painful, but I am grateful!

So after all of those rapes; wanting to kill people; going to jail, and trying to out run the police, my life really had become a living hell. I was feeling bad, looking bad, and getting tired of the ruthless people I was meeting on the street. I kept using and began to cry out to God for help like never before. During a conversation with my mother she said, "All this time I called myself helping you, and I realized I am only hurting you! I'm not going to continue to hurt you anymore. I'm going to stop doing for you like I have been doing." Hearing that really made me fearful for my life because I knew if my mom wasn't for me, who would be? Everyone else had already given up hope for me or at least they acted like it.

My sisters had stopped believing in me. My father didn't talk very much any way so he didn't have anything to say to me. Most of the time my children acted like I didn't exist. It was disturbing to see them cling to anyone besides me.

After being gone again for several days, I returned to my parent's house only to find a house full of people. I hurried to my room because I didn't want anyone to look at me in disgust. Grace ran in and out of my room and I tried to catch her and put her in the bed with me. I missed my children so much. Each time I grabbed her arm, she would break free. Once I caught her and placed her on top of my chest. All I wanted was a hug. She began to hit me and said, "Bad girl, bad, girl." I put her down and she ran out of the room. I didn't attempt to catch her again, as I was too busy crying and trying not to make too much noise. My feelings were hurt. I could not believe my two-year old knew that I was an unfit mother, and didn't want to have anything to do with me. I really was a bad girl and even Grace knew it.

I had become a basket case. During the day while at my mother's house she would give me food in a bag and send me away. She would tell me, "I will see you later." One particular night when she sent me away I felt so alone. I walked up the street in the dark to catch the bus. I stared out the window wondering what happened to my dreams and goals. How did I allow myself to get to this point in life? No one wanted me, not even the streets. I wanted to fall asleep somewhere and escape from reality.

Chapter 10
Back to Kentucky

It was the summer of 1987 and my mother was up to her schemes again. I know it had to be hard for a mother to watch her daughter go through such a terrible, unnecessary ordeal. All she wanted was for me to get myself together and take care of my children. She was always thinking of things she could do to help me. She often told me she prayed for my safety and her biggest fear was a knock on the door, and someone telling her I had been found dead.

My mom and my husband had arranged for me to take another trip to Kentucky for seven days. This time my children, Michael and Grace, were going with me. Someone purchased the airline tickets and we were scheduled to fly on Friday. Mom started making preparations for us to go. She purchased new clothes and made sure our hair was done. I was still smoking like crazy but was willing to go back to Kentucky. I remember it like it was yesterday.

I had put a pair of my shoes in the shop and they were supposed to be ready on Thursday. I had been smoking cocaine all week and needed to go pick them up. For some reason, mother trusted me to go by myself. When I arrived at the shoe shop the shoes weren't ready. I sat there for a few minutes and waited and they still weren't ready. I decided to go see my good friend up the street, the one who had to go to the library to clean himself. I went to his house to tell him bye. I really wanted to smoke a little too. I only had eight dollars to get my shoes out of the shop.

I was visiting with him and wishing he had some cocaine. We had a nice visit. He told me he was going to miss me. I gave him the eight dollars and asked him to go find us a hit. He put his shoes on and left. When he returned, he was empty handed. I was disappointed and relieved at the same time. There was a knock on the door. It was one of his friends, broke, and looking to get high. I asked him, "Do you know where to get anything from?" He said, "Yes." I told him, "I only have eight dollars, do you think you can get some?" He jumped up and left. I got nervous because he took too long to get back. I thought he had taken off with my money or got busted or something. When he finally came back, he told us that he went everywhere he knew of, and nobody had anything. Again, I was sad and relieved because I knew if I had been able to score any cocaine that evening, more than likely, I would have missed my flight the next day.

I left and went back to the shoe shop to get my shoes. When I got to the house my mother said, "What in the world took you so long to go and pick up some shoes?" I told her they were not ready and I went to say goodbye to my friend. She looked at me in disbelief.

Before you knew it, we were saying our goodbyes and off to Kentucky. The children were excited. It was Grace's first time flying, but Michael, Jr. had flown before. Michael couldn't wait to see his daddy. He loved his daddy and missed him since he was away in the military. Going to Kentucky to spend a week with his dad, was the greatest thing that could happen to him.

We stayed at the Hotel 8, on Kraft Street in Clarksville, Tennessee. We had a good time there. The children could swim all day if they wanted. They enjoyed eating Mc Donald's and having a good time. This day will always be unforgettable.

I got out of the water to take Grace to the bathroom. Out the blue, my husband asked me, "Will you stay here in Kentucky with me?" He really caught me off guard. I told him, "I don't know if I can do that." I went up to the room and sat down on the side of the bed while Grace went to the bathroom. While sitting there, I thought about the question my husband had just asked me. I was thinking to myself, "I cannot stay here, away from my mom, dad, sisters and friends! Oh no, I can't do that." Then, all of a sudden I heard this quiet, still voice say, "Isn't that what you prayed for?" I heard it again, "Isn't that what you prayed for? To get out of California?" This time I said to myself, "Yes!" By the time Grace came out of the bathroom, I was on the phone calling California.

My mother answered the phone, "Hello." I said, "Momma, guess what?" She said, "What!" "Michael asked me to stay here with him in Kentucky!" I said. She said, "Oh my God that's good!" Then she asked me, "What did you say?" I told her, "I told him yes." Then my baby sister got on the phone and she was crying, and she told me, "You need to come back home." I told her, "No, we were going to stay here." Then they suggested I send the children back while I got things together. It sounded like a really good idea but immediately I heard this voice say, "No, keep the children here with you. Don't work, but stay home with your children, because you have been separated for a long time." We all cried on the phone together.

We are a really close family. None of us had ever been apart from each for an extended period of time, but I knew they had to let me go if they didn't want to lose me. I told my children we were going to stay here in Kentucky. I was excited, scared, sad, relieved, and only God knows what else I was feeling at the time. Michael, Jr. didn't care about anything as long as he was going to be with his daddy. Grace was only two years old, so she didn't care as long as she felt loved, and that she did. We were all one big happy family.

Moving to Kentucky

I was over rejoicing and nervous at the same time. I was going to be reunited with my husband after almost ten years of separation. I was going to be living in a different place than what I was accustomed to. Being born and raised in Los Angeles, California, and coming to Kentucky was a real culture shock to me. I really liked it because it was laid back and the streets were not crowded like in Los Angeles. As far as everything else, it really did take some getting used to. When I made the decision to stay, I told the Lord, "I will stay as long as you allow me to go to Los Angeles often and visit my family."

Since we didn't have any family in Kentucky, the military community became our family. My husband had made some close connections with some guys. Everybody was willing to help each other. We stayed in the hotel for a week and my husband's friend allowed us to move into their house. It was a temporary situation. They really were nice people and had one small child. Although they told us we could stay with them as long as we needed, I knew better.

My husband was trying to find us a place to live. He worked every day and had to look for us a place to stay in the evening. I couldn't help him because I didn't have a clue where to go. One day he came home from work and said he had found us a trailer and it wasn't that bad. I had heard horror stories from his friend's wives and I wasn't going to stay in a trailer park. Now I know some trailer parks are really nice. That is why it is good to obtain information for yourself.

He went out apartment hunting again. He was only an E-2 in the Army and didn't make very much money at all. I wasn't working, so our income was limited. Finally, one day Michael came home from work and told me he found an apartment that rented for two hundred and something a month. I immediately asked him, "What does the place look like and where is it located?" He said, "In Oak Grove, Kentucky and it is not far from the base." The place we were staying was in Clarksville, Tennessee. In my mind, I could only imagine a small "chicken coop" for two hundred dollars a month. In California you couldn't rent any apartment for that price unless you were on section eight. He assured me it was really nice and I needed to go see it. So I told him we could go.

When we drove up I couldn't believe my eyes. It was very large and nice. It was called "Kentucky Manor." I liked the outside appearance of the complex. The manager (let's call her Cynthia) of the apartment was an extremely nice lady. She walked with us to the apartment. I preferred not to live in the back complex, but that was the only one available at the time. The rent was based on our income, which was excellent for us. We also qualified for vouchers to help get our utilities turned on. As we were nearing the apartment I was hoping it wasn't roach infested, but when she opened the door I was amazed at what I saw. It was a nice two-bedroom, downstairs apartment. The bedrooms were a nice size. I said smiling, "I really like it, how soon can we move in?" She told us, "It's ready, you can move in whenever you want to. When are the packers coming with your goods?" I told her, "This is it! We only came to Kentucky with our suitcases." She said, "That's it? You don't have any furniture or anything?" I told her, "No, no furniture or anything, just a few suit cases with our clothes."

She looked puzzled so I thought I better explain what our situation was. I told her, "You see, we came here for a vacation and then we decided to stay. California is our home. We are starting all over again." When she heard what was going on she asked me, "Would you like to go to the office to see if we have anything that you could use? When people abandon their apartments we seize their goods. We sell them as a means of recovering the rent." I told her, "Sure, I wouldn't mind taking a look around."

To my amazement, they had a room full of furniture. I was standing there in awe while the manager starting walking around picking up things she thought we could use. I told her, "Wait, wait, wait just a minute. How much are these things? We probably don't have enough money to pay for this now." She told me, "Don't worry about it. You can just pay me as you get the money. We can make some arrangements for you to get it paid for." I told her, "Okay."

She had a navy blue two-piece sectional sofa sleeper. She said, "This will be perfect for you. Your babies will not have to sleep on the floor." I said, "Oh good." Then she found a big bag of silver forks, knives and spoons. She also had a cream colored set of China. I loved the china, but I thought that it might be too expensive for us. She told me the price and I was shocked and I said, "We will take that too." By the time we finished, it had started to get dark but she didn't care. We took the furniture and the dishes over to the apartment that night. We didn't have a dinner table, or a TV, but we were happy and content.

I did manage to go back to Los Angeles to get rid of the things I wasn't going to take back to Kentucky. The kids had a lot of toys, but we couldn't take everything they owned. I didn't stay in California long because I had to get back to put my son in school. It was and still is a sad time when I have to leave my family and come back to Kentucky. Surprising to me, when I went back home to Los Angeles, I didn't use drugs nor, did I have the urge to use them. This was a Miracle!

Chapter 16 Total Deliverance

It was amazing how I could take a flight from California to Kentucky, and be instantly delivered from a cocaine and drug habit that spanned for almost ten years! I had heard about deliverance but I had not experienced it before. How did it really work? During the last ten years prior to that day, my family and friends had been praying for me. I had been, on occasion, praying for myself. There were many times I asked the Lord to change me or just let me die in the street to put me out of my misery. I knew if I had to live the rest of my life as a drug addict, I would rather be dead. The day I took that flight to Kentucky, for what I thought was a one-week vacation, turned out to be MY FLIGHT INTO MY DESTINY!

I had no idea when I landed in Nashville, Tennessee and was driven to Fort Campbell, Kentucky I would have a life altering experience. My plans were to have a good time in Kentucky with the children and my husband, and fly back home to what I was used to. God had another plan!

I was instantly delivered from cocaine. I have never had a desire to smoke again and I have never had to fight the temptation of using cocaine or any other drug. The craving for cocaine, marijuana, uppers, downers, and hallucinogenic drugs has miraculously gone away forever! I didn't have the longing to go to the nightclubs, despite my love for dancing and partying.

Supernaturally, the desire was gone forever. It seemed like in a few hours, my life had drastically changed. I must admit, I was wondering how long would this change last. How long would it be before I was back out on the streets getting high? I heard there were places in Hopkinsville, Kentucky to get drugs, but I had also heard there were a lot of places in Hopkinsville where soldiers were not allowed to go. I had no interest in going to Hopkinsville for any reason because I knew if I started using cocaine again I would be out of control. The drugs would rule me.

The wonderful thing is, since 1987, my desire has been to go to church and do the right things in life! I was still smoking cigarettes and drinking a little alcohol on occasion, but it wasn't long until I was delivered from drinking completely. In November of 1987, I was delivered from cigarettes. It is amazing, simply amazing to me!

There are many stories in the Bible where people had suffered for many, many years, but when they came in contact with Jesus, their lives were changed in an instant. For example, the woman in the Bible, who was crippled for eighteen years, yet Jesus set her free. "On a Sabbath Jesus was teaching in one of the synagogues, and a woman was there who had been crippled by a spirit for eighteen years. She was bent over and could not straighten up at all. When Jesus saw her, he called her forward and said to her, Woman, you are set free from your infirmity. Then he put his hands on her, and immediately she straightened up and praised God" (Luke 13:10-13).

There are several stories of Jesus setting people free once and for all. He did it for them, I'm a witness he did it for me, and I can testify he will do the same for you! At the time I realized I wasn't craving drugs, I hadn't got a full understanding of what was going on with me, but I knew I would eventually. I didn't know I was fully delivered until time passed.

New Desires

I re-dedicated my life back to the Lord. I wanted to live a Christian life again and teach my children to do the same. While we were in the process of finding a good church, we would have church at home with the television ministries. I told the Lord I wouldn't go out of the house unless I really needed to and I wanted Him to make sure only those who meant us good came in. I was afraid of meeting the wrong people and possibly getting into trouble. I prayed that prayer and I took the consecrated oil and wiped it across the doorframe and "Plead the Blood" of Jesus over it. God answered my prayer. When I tell this story, some people say, "Girl you were crazy." I had no reason to leave the house very much, so I didn't.

I can recall a time in California when I was in the grocery store minding my own business and this guy asked me, "Do you want to go and get high?" Those situations like that made me wonder, how in the world did he know I used drugs? Out of all of the people in the store, why did he ask me that question? I don't know, but it was that type of behavior I didn't want repeated.

Unless I absolutely had to, I wouldn't go outside if my husband or son weren't at home. I wouldn't even go to the front of our complex to check the mail. I waited until they got home. Grace had to play in the house until her brother got home. I had a lot of neighbors and I was cordial when I saw them, but I wouldn't tarry. This went on for a short while until one day I said to myself, "I need to let this baby go outside and play for just a little while!" I prayed and said to the Lord, "I need to meet one good friend." I quickly changed my prayer to "One good Christian friend." That was all I wanted.

I thought about taking a book outside to read while Grace played. I wondered if the other ladies would get the hint I did not want to be bothered. One day I got the nerve to try it. We went to the park, which was located in the middle of the apartment complex. Grace was swinging, having a really good time, and I was sitting down reading my book. No one was around to bother me and that was good.

Suddenly, I heard a little girl running around saying, "Land in the Name of Jesus, Land in the Name of Jesus!" I wanted to look up, but I just kept on reading. Again, I heard her say, "Land in the Name of Jesus." Only this time she ran in front of me, almost stepping on my foot. I looked up briefly and saw an adorable Caucasian girl who looked to be about ten years old. She had the biggest smile on her face as she glanced at me. She never stopped moving though, she just kept saying, "Land butterfly, in the Name of Jesus, land!" As she spun around and began running away I said to myself, "Lord! I wonder who her mother is? I would like to meet her, surely she must be saved!"

I sat there a little while longer before Grace and I headed back to the house. As we walked to the apartment, I was thanking God that nothing happened to me. I was still amazed about the little girl and the butterfly!

I Saw Jesus in You

The door swung open as my son ran inside screaming, "Momma, momma you got to come quick!" As I ran to the door, I was shouting, "What! What's wrong?" "You got to come quick and see my friend! She got hurt on the bus!" I immediately put on my shoes and ran out of the house with him. We ran all the way to one of the apartments in the front of the complex. When we got to the apartment, Michael began banging on the door as I tried to catch my breath. A Caucasian lady opened the door and beside her stood the same little girl that was telling the butterfly to land in the name of Jesus. She wasn't smiling like she was in the park the other day. She looked sad and had tears in her eyes. There was a cut on her forehead, right between her eyes with blood oozing down her face. Before I knew it, I dropped down on my knees, wrapped my arms around her, and began praying for her like she was my own daughter. I prayed and I wept.

I stood up and apologized for doing that. I did it without permission or hesitation. The woman at the door smiled and said to me, "That's okay baby, I thank you for praying for my daughter!" As I listened to her, a man appeared in the hallway about seven feet from where we were. She said, "Hi, I am Carol and this is my little girl, Jamie. That's my husband, Jim, and he's holding our baby Rebecca!" I extended my hand and said, "Hi I'm Sha Jackson. I'm Michael's mom! He told me his friend was hurt so I came right away." Carol said, "Thank you, I appreciate it. We were just getting ready to take Jamie to the hospital." I then asked, "Would you like for me to watch your little girl, Rebecca?" Carol said, "Sure baby, that would be a great idea!" Immediately her husband spoke up and politely said, "No! That's okay! Thank you anyway, but we'll just take her with us." Carol stood smiling at me and she agreed with her husband and she thanked me again for coming. I told her, "If you need me for anything, just let me know and I will help you if I can." "Okay, thank you!" she said.

My son and I walked back to our apartment. When we got home my husband asked me what happened and I explained everything to him. He asked, "Do you know those people?" I said, "No." He replied, "And you expected her to leave her baby with you?" I told him, "She was going to do it until her husband said no." What my husband didn't realize was, when I went to that house and I looked at the little girl standing there bleeding, it was as if I already knew them. We didn't treat each other like strangers. I later found out that our spirits knew each other. She was a Christian and also the lady assigned by God to disciple me.

Carol and I became the best of friends. I prayed I would be able to meet that little girl's mom, but I didn't have a clue it would happen like that. A few days later, Carol came down to our apartment. She had drawn me a picture and thanked me again for praying for her daughter. In the picture was a little girl standing with a lady on her knees hugging her, and a woman standing beside her. Above the picture she wrote, “When I saw you, I saw Jesus!” I didn’t know what to say to her. I was thinking to myself, “She saw Jesus in me?” I invited her into the house. She came in, but didn’t stay long. That was the beginning of a long friendship with Carol. She was the best friend I had prayed for.

Front and Center

My family and I started going to “Assembly of God Church” in Clarksville, Tennessee. Most of the time, I caught a ride to church with Carol because we didn’t have a car big enough for all of us. We often arrived late because Carol had no sense of time. I didn’t want to be late, but as long as I got there I was happy. Even though service had already started, we would walk down the center aisle to find a seat on the front row. I know folks say when you enter a place late it is rude to walk to the front. I had been out of church so long, I was glad to be back. I didn’t care who talked about me; I wanted the front seat! I couldn’t understand if you were on time to church, why wouldn’t you take a seat front and center? That would seem like the right thing to do to me. It was a blessing to me to arrive at church late and still be able to find a good seat. I’m not saying we didn’t try and get to church on time, but every Sunday we were late! This went on for years.

Church was always a blessing. Mr. Jones was the pastor when we started attending and Brother Montoya was the assistant pastor. We went on Sunday nights from time to time to hear him preach. He was a good minister also. I really liked Assembly of God and I met some wonderful people while attending there. Every Saturday night Brother Montoya, without fail, would call me and invite us to come to Sunday school. I would always say, "Okay, we will try and be there." I think I was only able to go to Sunday school twice! I admired Brother Montoya's faithfulness. He never ceased to call me while I attended that church.

It seemed every Sunday Pastor Jones would talk about his brother who died of emphysema. It ministered to me because I always had a pack of cigarettes in my purse. I recall one Sunday when he began talking about his brother; I had to push my purse under the pew in front me because my cigarettes were visible. I could hardly wait to get out of church so I could smoke. One Sunday in particular, we were driving home. I didn't like to smoke in front of Carol and the kids, but sometimes I just couldn't resist. I asked Carol if could smoke and she said, "Sure baby fire up!" I felt so relieved. It felt good to be able to smoke and rest my nerves. I remember asking Carol a question about something and as she began to answer she reminded me of what the Bible said. She always did that.

She couldn't answer a single question without including the Bible. I couldn't understand that. As I was blowing the smoke out of the window into the crisp morning air, I remember saying to myself, "Does she always have to talk about the word of God? I mean I want to hear the word, but all of the time do I have to hear it? Sometimes I just wanted an answer from her without hearing about the Bible."

One night, she called me to tell me something. It led to her wanting to show me something in the word (Bible). When Carol would go to a scripture, she wouldn't just read a verse or two, she would read you four or five chapters. I am not kidding! Sometimes she would read to me so much I would fall asleep on her and start snoring. I would snore so loud I would wake myself up and realize I was still on the phone and she was still reading! I would say, "Carol, I am so sorry I fell asleep on you again." She would say, "That's okay baby, I was just feeding your spirit." She would continue reading if I let her, and she wouldn't stop until she reached the end.

Carol did this all the time until one day I was talking to her, and the word began to come out of my mouth. I caught myself and wondered what I was saying. Carol said, "That's okay baby, see the word is getting in you!" I was shocked. I needed the word to change me. I was saved but I needed a lot of work done on myself. I was messed up from all the years of abuse and trauma. I was a mess inside and out! My husband was a mess too.

It didn't take long before my husband started showing his true color. I thought he had changed, but he had only gotten worse. Being in the military disciplined him in some areas, but he still needed a lot of help. He did manage to go to work everyday and that is one thing he didn't do when we first got married. He was doing a lot of drinking with his Army buddies. They would start on Thursday and wouldn't stop until Sunday. At the time, I was drinking a little bit, but I wasn't getting drunk. I drank wine coolers occasionally, but my husband drank beer until he passed out. This wasn't uncommon. Actually, the majority of the soldiers did the same thing, yet they went to work each morning and did their job.

I didn't like for my husband to drink because he would say rude and nasty things to me. He hurt my feelings many times. I wondered why I put myself back in this predicament. People would tell me, "He didn't mean what he was saying." But I always heard that a drunk doesn't lie. He would wait until he was drunk and curse me. I can't stand for someone to curse at me. I know I was supposed to be saved, but I wasn't fully delivered. Sometimes I would scream and curse him back. I would use profanity to the fullest! It felt good while I was doing it because it would cause him to back off, but afterwards, I felt bad. I would have to ask God for forgiveness.

A War in My Members

Romans 7:14-25

Carol told me that my spirit wanted to be obedient to the word of God, but my flesh wanted to do its own thing. Actually, it wanted to do everything that was contrary to the word of God. That day, she helped me understand the struggle going on inside of me. I really needed more of the word but I could only do so much. I desired to do right but my husband seemed to bring out the worst in me. I didn't know it then, but that was just what I needed to do. Everything that wasn't like Christ needed to come out of me. To make matters worse, at night he would expect me to come together with him as if nothing ever happened. He would pick a fight and then ask me to forgive him and make love to him. What he didn't realize was I was having a hard time sleeping with him.

Whether we fought or not, sex was a terrible thing for me. I knew it was because of the rapes and my experiences with so many different men. It made me nauseated. This night in particular, I couldn't fake it. I could hardly wait for him to finish. I immediately jumped up, ran to the bathroom and threw up. He came running in the bathroom asking me, "What's wrong with you?" I explained to him, "It is really hard for me to have sex because it reminds me of all the abuse I have been through. Every single time we make love I have to re-live the trauma. EVERY-TIME! It makes me gag sometimes, throw up sometimes and almost every time I cry."

He apologized, but of course, he would want to do it anyway. He would be satisfied and I would be petrified. Sometimes he would ask me, "Are you just lying there?" "I can't do anything!" I said. Sex wasn't pleasurable for me. It was haunting! I prayed about it because I wanted to please my husband. I often speculated why he was staying with me and dealing with this. I did have a lot of issues, but I was trying to work through them.

I read my Bible and prayed everyday. I prayed about everything. I had read in the Bible, "In all thy ways acknowledge him and he will direct your path" (Proverbs 3:6 NKJV). I had it bad. If the kids wanted to go out and play, I prayed about it first. If I had peace, I would let them go, if not, they didn't go out. I was trying to walk the Christian walk. I got down on my knees and prayed and got upset because I couldn't pray for an hour straight. I would ask God over and over what was wrong with me.

My sister Santa called and I asked her why couldn't I pray like I heard other people. No matter how hard I tried to pray long, I fell asleep and woke up with sore knees. Santa told me, "First, prayer is a discipline, then it is a desire, then it is a delight! You are in discipline stage and that stage is difficult." I would often wonder how long this stage was going to last. Eventually, I was able to pray more than fifteen minutes on my knees, and then I was able to pray for an hour.

Discouragement

The enemy always let me know how wrong, unworthy and unholy I really was. He often tried to make me feel like a total loser. He would say things like, "Look at you, you can't do anything right! You might as well go back to using drugs. You are nothing but a sick loser anyway." I had to fight through these feelings every week. I thank God for His word and my sisters calling and encouraging me. My sister, Santa, was really connected to me in the beginning of my recovery. I would rehearse different thoughts in my mind and she would sense it in her spirit and call from California to minister to me over the phone. I guess God used her most because she was the one who could really relate to my struggle. She too had been a drug user, but only for a short period of time. She told me, "Use the word of God to encourage yourself in the Lord."

When the enemy told me I couldn't or I wouldn't, I would tell myself that I could. I learned a scripture that says, "I can do everything through Him (Christ) who gives me strength" Philippians 4:13 NKJV. I would also often quote, "Therefore, there is now no condemnation for those who are in Christ Jesus, who do not walk according to the flesh, but according to the Spirit" (Romans 8:1 NKJV). I had to quote these scriptures all the time because the enemy was trying to mess with my mind. He was trying to get me to give up, but no matter how much it hurt and how much of a failure I thought I was, I had to learn to stand on the word of God. There were many days when I felt all alone but the word of God said, "He would never leave me nor forsake me" (Hebrews 13:5b NKJV). I knew as long as I didn't leave Him, He wasn't going to leave me. All I had to do was hold on and not let go, no matter what.

Holding on was a job in itself. Giving up was so much easier, and it was something I was oh so familiar with. I knew how to give up real well, but now I was in a place in my life where that wasn't optional. I had to hold on to God's unchanging hand until the work was complete. I knew I was a work in progress and the polishing wasn't comfortable. As much as I wanted to give up, I didn't. I realized I had to learn how to fight in the spirit.

Chapter 11
I'll Teach You How to Fight

Fighting in the spirit was different than fighting in the flesh. I knew how to fight in the flesh although I didn't like to. I fought to defend myself or someone else, but to fight in the spirit meant taking on a whole new attitude. When I began to fight in the spirit with the word of God, I came up against everything I was used to doing. I had to hold back all of my feelings and emotions and learn how to line them up with the word of God. This wasn't easy to do, but I was willing to take on the struggle to accomplish the goal. All I had was the word. I really didn't have many friends and I didn't trust my judgment of character because of my past. There were many, many days I would fall on my face and cry out to God to help me make it through.

God spoke to me and told me my current marriage arrangement was just like when we first got married. I wanted to live for the Lord and my husband didn't. We were like hot and cold, night and day, negative and positive! The Lord told me, "If you do what I tell you to do, this time, you will win and not lose. You will not fight in the flesh, but in the spirit!"

Four Hours a Day

As a stay-at-home mom, I had a schedule. Each morning I got my husband off to work, my son off to school, cooked breakfast for my little girl and cleaned the house. I prepared lunch for Grace and sometimes my husband if he came home. I cleaned again and let my daughter play awhile. When she went down for a nap I was able to enjoy some "me time." I got to watch soap operas in peace. It was my quiet time. I watched television from 11am to 3pm. Afterwards, I had to get ready for my son to come home from school and my husband to come home from work, if he wasn't in the field. I tried not to let anything interfere with the time I had set aside for myself.

One day, the Lord told me to get in the word and study for four hours a day. I said, "What?" I thought to myself, "When am I going to find the time to study for four hours a day?" The Lord quietly spoke to me, "The four hours you have set aside to watch television, turn the television off and use that time to study!" I couldn't believe my ears!

Of course I walked in disobedience for several days. The entire time I was watching my soaps, I felt so guilty for not doing what I was told. One day I decided to be obedient. I kept the same routine and substituted watching television for studying the word of God. I really thought it was going to be a chore, but it was enjoyable.

Once I sat down and began to read and cross-reference the Bible, I was surprised at how the time passed. I wanted to read more and more because of interesting things I was learning. It was amazing how God waited until I worked out my quiet time. He even let me perfect my schedule where I hardly had any interruptions. I guess He said if I wait for her to set aside time for what she wants to do, she will have no excuse when I ask her to replace it with what I want her to do. I knew it was what I needed to be doing, but did I want to do it? NO! Believe it or not, I never got involved in the soaps again. I had no desire for them anymore. I found I could live without them and the word was what I needed more than anything else at that time.

I did a lot of journaling along with my Bible studying. It was really great for me and it saved my life. God began to show me how to have the right spirit. It even taught me how I was supposed to reflect and meditate. Was I able to do everything right away? No, but I knew what was right and wrong and the holy spirit would always put a finger on me when I was out of order. I was still smoking cigarettes when I was studying, but I studied nonetheless.

No More Cigarettes

I started to get sick at night. I smoked during the day but at bedtime, I coughed and had dry heaves. This continued for almost an hour and then I was able to go to sleep. Night after night this happened. It got to the point I couldn't take it anymore, but I also couldn't stop smoking. I began to pray to God for help to quit. I also was reminded of Pastor Jones' brother who died of emphysema. I prayed and I smoked, and I smoked and I prayed. One day I told myself, "This is it! I am not going to smoke anymore." I put the pack in the kitchen sink that was filled with dishwater, and then I threw the pack in the trash. Later that day I went into the trash can and got them out. I carefully took a wet cigarette out of the package trying not to tear it. I went to the stove and rolled the cigarette over the eye of the stove until dried. I got the lighter and I fired it up and I pulled long, hard and steady. It was so wonderful! It was so good I smoked the whole cigarette. After I smoked I felt so bad. I had to repent and pray again because I felt like a loser. I continued to smoke for a few days until I tried to quit again. I wasn't smoking as many because of the coughing at night, but I was still smoking.

My husband was in the field and we didn't have a car so I had no way to go get cigarettes. This was the perfect time to quit. I finally ran out of cigarettes, but when I couldn't fight the urge anymore, I asked my neighbor to go get me some. He told me that he wasn't coming back for a while so I asked him if he would take me to the store and I would walk back to the house.

I had been without a cigarette for a few days at this point. I went inside the store and got the eggs and cigarettes. I was smoking Benson and Hedges menthol at the time. The store was located on 41A in Oak Grove. 41A is a very busy road. The speed limit is 45mph. As I was walking through the parking lot heading towards the street to walk back to the house, I fired up that menthol cigarette. I pulled long and hard on it. I held it and then I blew it out. I will never forget it. I was coming upon a large light pole in the parking lot near the road. I felt like I was going to black out. I was trying to grab Grace but I couldn't. I felt like I was fading fast. I barely made it to the light pole and sat down. I know I was out for a few seconds. I was rendered helpless. I couldn't help my daughter or myself. I wanted to grab her so she wouldn't run into the busy street but I couldn't. I gained consciousness and I looked around wondering what happened to me. I was so glad to see that Grace was still there and nothing had happened to her. All I could say was, "Thank you Lord!"

After getting myself together, I grabbed Grace by the hand and we started walking home. We had a long way to go to get to the house. It didn't seem that long when I wanted that cigarette, but now that I had to make the hike back to the house I couldn't believe how far we had to go. The 911 Hwy is a two-lane road without sidewalks. The speed limit was 35mph. We had to walk in the street most of the way. "Oh my God what in the world was I thinking about?" A lady pulled in front of me and parked. As we approached her, she rolled her window down and asked me if I needed a ride. I declined, thinking it wasn't that far. She said, "Where are you going?" I said "To Kentucky Manor Apartments?" She said, "That's a long way, its no problem for me do take you there!" I really didn't want to walk any further with Grace. I got in the car, but I sat the eggs and Grace on my lap. I said to myself, "God help her if she tries anything."

Getting in that car brought back bad memories. I could hardly wait to get out! She was trying to have small talk with me and I believe I was so scared I was speechless. All I wanted was to get home and get back in my house. She talked the whole way home and I couldn't tell you what she talked about. I told her, "Thank You." I got out of her car, and we came real close to running to get back in the house.

I was so relieved to be back at home. I thanked God for keeping us safe while walking on that road trying to get a cigarette that I didn't need. A few weeks later God took the desire for cigarettes away. I didn't want to smoke anymore. It was sometime in November of 1987. I don't recall the exact day because when I finally realized I had not smoked a cigarette, it had been a few days. God delivered me and I didn't know it. I told God, "You are so smooth." I was glad it was finally over.

One night my husband had some of his friends over and we were playing spades. Everyone at the table was smoking cigarettes except me. My husband looked at me and asked, "How can you sit here with all of this smoke and not want a cigarette?" I looked at him after taking a minute to think about it and said, "Because when God delivers you from something, it is as if you have never done it before!" In amazement he said, "You mean to tell me that you don't have any urge to smoke?" I said, "I am not thinking about a cigarette. I actually don't have the desire and I don't have to fight back any cravings either." It was over for me. Just like the cocaine was over, the cigarette smoking was over too! Finally the taste for cigarettes was gone!

Thanksgiving Dinner

Thanksgiving Day was fast approaching and we still didn't have a dinette set. We either sat on the floor or the couch to eat our food. I prayed and asked God for a table so we wouldn't have to eat our first Thanksgiving dinner as a family on the floor.

One day I was compelled to go to a furniture store I heard about in Hopkinsville to see if I could find a table. I told my husband what my intentions were and of course he said, "We don't have the money to buy a table." I said, "I just want to go see what they have and what the prices are." I wasn't thinking about layaway, but when I found a table that I really liked, that was our only option. I asked her, "What do we need to put it on layaway?" It seemed like forever, but the day finally came when we were able to pick up the table. We sat around the table for dinner. It was truly a Happy Thanksgiving as we gathered around our new dinette set!

We had a lot of company for the holiday. Many of my husband's friends from work came over. We had an abundance of food. Everyone pitched in and I did a lot of cooking. I had never prepared a traditional Thanksgiving dinner by myself. I called my mother to get all of her recipes. I called her several more times to ask her how to prepare them. It was a challenge, but by the grace of God, I got it all done. It wasn't as good as my mother's cooking, but everyone enjoyed it. I made a three-layer coconut pineapple cake. Some made fun of it because it was leaning to the side. But after tasting it, they didn't care if it leaned or not. It was good! The icing alone on this cake is very intimidating but I mastered it on this day. I remember taking lots of photos because I was so thankful. I was proud of myself for finally doing something on my own, and doing it right for a change.

Everyone enjoyed the day and we talked about doing it again next year. Christmas was fast approaching. For those of us who were going to be in town, we talked about spending Christmas together.

Christmas, oh my goodness! As a child I was accustomed to having very large gatherings with many gifts. I couldn't imagine what kind of Christmas we were going to have away from our family. I was so attached to them. Realistically, if I was in California and I was on drugs, I wouldn't spend too much time with them, but it is just the fact of not being home. We had thought about going home for Christmas but couldn't afford four plane tickets. We were poor as ducks! I accepted spending Christmas in Kentucky and had to make the best of it. I became very creative.

I got assistance from my sisters and parents. They were all very supportive of me and I couldn't wish for a better family. I am certain they were happy and relieved to know that their sister was on her way to becoming a normal person again. I know they were hoping and praying daily that my change was a permanent one, but at the time nobody knew, not even me. We all took it one day at time. All I could do was thank the good Lord for one more day of being clean and sober. Everyday though, it seemed as if I was learning another lesson.

I had so much to learn and so much to be delivered from. I didn't know how messed up I had become. It was a miracle that I was still clothed and in my right mind. I will try to recount the days of my deliverance to you. I came to realize once we are saved, we need to get delivered from things that so easily get us off course. I had to take off "Me" and put on more of Christ everyday. It wasn't easy but because I was willing it was possible. I was able to do the things I needed to do in order to survive and be successful. One day I learned about the "Spirit behind the man"

Spirit Behind the Man

One day my husband came home in rare form, as he often did. This particular day my girlfriend, Carol, was visiting me. My husband started arguing with me and cursing me about something I don't even recall. He misbehaved in such a manner and wasn't concerned that my friend was there. I stood and looked at him until I just couldn't take it any longer. It was the cursing and name-calling that was unbearable. It reminded me of when I was on the streets. I couldn't stand to be degraded.

Imagine being home all day and your husband walks in the house looking three shades darker than normal with small dark piercing eyes and starts yelling for no apparent reason. I tried to calm him and asked what was wrong, but he continued to curse and accuse me. I started cursing back at him. At this point, we are yelling back and forth and in each other's face so close I could tell he had been drinking. His behavior was inexcusable.

I was becoming furious and I think my friend, Carol, could tell. As we shouted nasty words at each other, Carol leaned over and began whispering in my ear, "We wrestle not against flesh and blood..." At that moment I remember taking my eyes off of my husband and looking at her as if to say, "What are you saying to me?" Then my husband started yelling at me again. I looked away from Carol and looked at him again and started cursing him. Carol leaned into my ear again and said; "We wrestle not against flesh and blood but against principalities…" Again I stopped yelling at my husband and looked at her until he yelled at me again. This went on for a while and then I looked at Carol and she said, "Come on baby, it is not him." I looked back at my husband and I left the house quickly because I was at the point of making physical contact and he seemed ready to do the same. I stormed out of the house and Carol was with me.

All I can remember is her riding me around town and my screaming. I couldn't believe that he had done this to me again. I was hurting so much until I felt like I was going to have a heart attack. He was hurting me so bad and I couldn't hurt him back. I really wanted to but I knew that it wasn't God's way of handling things. All I could do was scream.

I screamed and cried and Carol prayed and drove that little car around and around until I calmed down enough for her to take me back home. I know I probably frightened her because I believe that was the first time she had witnessed my outburst. I thanked God for her. If she had not been there that day, I don't know what would have transpired. God knew; that is why He had her there.

After I calmed down she was able to minister to me and help me understand what was going on and what I needed to do to avoid the same trap again. Carol told me a lot of things that night, but the one thing I want to share that she told me is, "It is not the man but it is the spirit behind the man and that is why we wrestle not against flesh and blood, but against principalities, against powers, against the rulers of the darkness of this world, against spiritual wickedness in high places" Ephesians 6:12 (King James Version).

By Carol explaining this scripture to me, it helped me to understand what was going on with my husband. The enemy was using him to try to get to me. That is why he didn't look like himself when he came into the house. From that day forward, every time that happened to me, I had a choice to make. Either I was going to fight him back in the flesh, flesh against flesh, or I was going to stay in the spirit and fight spirit against spirit. I have to confess, sometimes I chose to fight him in the flesh and when I did, I found myself face down on the floor crying out to God because I knew I had made the wrong choice. I had to repent and ask God for forgiveness. This gave my husband something to boast about because every time I messed up, my husband would throw it in my face. "You're no different from me or anybody else, you're only human and you have problems too!" Unfortunately he didn't understand this wasn't a game of win or lose for me; it was a matter of life and death! I don't know why he thought I was trying to be better than anybody else. It was about SURVIVAL to me!

I was determined to survive and doing so meant going God's way. The more I prayed about the situation, the more God revealed to me what the enemy was trying to do to me through my husband. My job was to love Michael, Sr. unconditionally and pray him through; his job was to drive me to the point of destruction. This was new to me because my way of handling things was to simply remove myself from it. It wasn't the will of God for my life right now. I didn't fully understand what was going on but I was willing to stay in it and try and work this thing out. Every day seemed like a new lesson learned. After my husband would do something like this to me then he would offer an apology and I was supposed to accept it. Then, of course, he wanted to make love to me like nothing ever happened.

I had to forgive him, as much as I didn't want to, I had to. I was relieved to know it wasn't my husband and it was the evil spirit of the enemy that was using him to get to me AGAIN!! Of course, it was out to destroy him also.

Pray In the Spirit

Why was my husband treating me this way? I couldn't do anything right. He always had something to complain about. One day he came home for lunch. I had it already prepared and waiting on him. Meanwhile, I had started preparing dinner. I was standing at the stove cooking and he came in the house and sat down behind me cursing like a drunken sailor. I didn't respond outwardly, but on the inside I was cringing. He wanted to argue with me. He had been at work and I had not spoken to him since he left that morning. I did everything I knew to do as far as being a good wife. I repeatedly asked myself "Why did he ask me to come here and stay with him?" I often thought I didn't hear God correctly, and had made a huge mistake. All I wanted to do was bring him joy and be a part of his life. If he didn't want me here, he should let me know. If this is where God says I need to be, then why am I catching so much hell trying to be in the will of God? I couldn't understand what was going on!

I was stirring the food in the pot and he sat behind me arguing. I remembered what Santa told me one day. She said, "When he attacks you like that again you begin to pray in the spirit and he will either cut up or he will shut up!" I decided to try it that day to see if it worked. Quietly I began to pray in the Holy Ghost, which is speaking in tongues, and to my amazement it really did work. I never looked back at him while he was arguing. Out of the blue, he said to me, "Wait a minute, let me start over. Hi, how are you doing? How has your day been?" I had to stop for a minute and give God thanks and praise. I couldn't believe it. It really did work! After a brief moment of praising God inwardly I then turned around and spoke to him. After he left to go back to work, I began to pray to God. I was beginning to understand what God was trying to teach me. It was a battle in the spirit! Not fighting the battle in the flesh makes a big difference. I will discuss more on the Holy Spirit later. I praised God! Oh yes, I had learned the Power of Praise too.

Power of Praise

One night I was invited to New Birth Jerusalem Church in Clarksville, Tennessee to hear a preacher I had heard speak before. I enjoyed his ministry.

I went there expecting to hear him and go home. I had not participated in this type of service before. During the praise and worship part of the service, I thought the people were never going to stop praising God and get on with the service. I shouted and danced for a little while but then I was tired, it was getting late, and honestly, I had begun to get upset. I thought, "All of this is uncalled for! Don't they realize it's a weeknight and people need to go home?" Finally, they took their seats and we were able to hear a word from the preacher. The next day during my time of Bible study I remember asking the Lord what I should read that day. I picked up the Bible and thumbed through the pages, stopping in the book of Acts Chapter 16. As I read that day I learned how powerful praise was because Paul and Silas praised God when they were thrown into prison, and supernatural things began to happen.

After the lesson that day, I have never had a problem with praise. God heard me murmuring in my heart that night and he knew I didn't understand so he wasted no time making sure I got a good understanding of the power of praise! I don't complain anymore, I just join in. I believe when we don't comprehend things, we don't feel the need to do them. When I teach or encourage others, I try to make sure they have a good understanding, because I know if they don't, they will not see the purpose or significance of it. The Bible says "Wisdom is the principal thing; therefore get wisdom. And in all your getting, get understanding." Proverbs 4:7 (New King James Version). I thank God for helping me understand. Praise is not just something that the saints do when the music sounds good. I know now that praise is powerful and God inhabits the praises of his people. I'm not talking about just standing there and singing or clapping, with you mind wondering everywhere, but truly entering into the spirit realm. I know that I can praise God anytime I feel the need or desire to do so, and not just at church on Sunday or whenever there is a church service. But I didn't always know this.

Chapter 15 Living on Post

I remember getting the call to move on post. I left home to go somewhere, but had to run back in the house. The phone rang. I answered it hastily. It was the housing office. I had been praying and believing God for a house on post in Pierce Village. Moving on post was going to make life easier for us financially and my husband would be closer to work. We had been on the waiting list for quite some time and today was finally the day. I was pleased to get the call until she told me the house was in Lee Village. I didn't want to live in Lee Village. I asked her if I could pretend I didn't get the call and wait for a house in Pierce Village. She told me, "No, if you don't accept this house, I will have to bump you to the bottom of the list and it will be a while before you get another call back." Reluctantly, I accepted the house in Lee Village. I was given the address so I went by to look at it. I was so grateful to be on post, yet saddened I didn't get the housing area I had been praying and believing God for. I complained about it often.

One day a friend (let's call her Karen) told me to claim the house I wanted. I found an empty apartment in Pierce Village. I walked around it, prayed, and ran back to the car before someone saw me. A year later we got a call from housing, they informed us our apartment had come up for renovations and we had to relocate. I asked, "Where are we going to be moving?" She said, "Pierce Village." I started praising God on the phone. She told me I could go and look at it first before I accept it. I told her, "I already know that's what I want, but I will go and look at it first."

I learned sometimes God takes you around the block to get to your blessing. It was part of the process. Moving on post is what I prayed for and getting the housing area I wanted was an added bonus. God never told me he wasn't going to let us move into Pierce Village. I just needed to go by way of Lee Village first! We lived in Pierce Village a little over two years and I loved every moment of it. Many of my friends didn't like Pierce Village but the location and the house was perfect for us. We had no problems and I thanked God the whole time we lived there. It was perfect! It was great!

One beautiful sunny Saturday morning I was decorating Grace's room. I decided to put the stuffed animals all over her walls because she had so many. One thumbtack was difficult to get in the wall. While pushing it I injured my thumb. It was throbbing and the pain was unbearable. In tears, I went down stairs and told my husband what happened. He got some gauze and said it would be best if he wrapped it for me. It hurt so bad I wouldn't let him touch my thumb. I couldn't do anything without my thumb hurting. It was a beautiful day outside and I had planned to clean the house and run some errands. I couldn't do anything. I knew I should have gone to the hospital, but I didn't want to wait all day long. After sitting on the couch for a while pondering what I could do with this throbbing sore thumb, I decided to drive to the post office and get the mail. I had to drive pretty far. I carefully got up and I told my husband what I was attempting to do and he asked me, "Are you sure you can drive?" I said, "I should be all right, I'm only going to use one hand. I will be right back." He said, "Okay." Even with my one hand resting on the steering wheel, it still hurt.

The post office was near the hospital and I thought about going to the emergency room to see if it was crowded. Instead I got the mail and headed back home. In horrendous, excruciating pain I started driving. On my way home I had to pass Karen's house. She loved to pray and I remembered that the Bible says, "I also tell you this: If two of you agree here on earth concerning anything you ask, my Father in heaven will do it for you. For where two or three gather together as my followers, I am there among them." Matthew 18:19-20 New Living Translation (NLV). I believed that if we touched and agreed in prayer the situation should change.

Because Karen was more mature in the Lord than I was, I figured she knew what to do. She started off praying and then she started praising God and dancing all around the living room. I was standing there afraid to move because I didn't know what to do. I stood there and continued to pray and praise God. My thumb limited my movements. Karen continued to praise Him. It was hard to believe she was praising God like that for me. You would think that she was praying for herself or someone in her family. I mean she kept on and on and on and so I asked God, "What am I suppose to do?" and I heard him say, "Clap" I said, "Clap? You know I can't clap because my thumb hurts too bad." I heard him again say, "Clap!" I said to myself, "I will motion my hands like I am clapping but I can't actually clap because it will hurt too bad."

I began moving my hands towards each other as if I was going to clap, but I didn't let them touch. When I did this, I did feel some pain but I continued on. Karen was still shouting and dancing like she had just won a million dollars. I was praising Him out loud, and I heard the Lord say, "Let them touch." I said, "What!" Before I knew it, I was letting my hands touch and it wasn't hurting at all. I started to clap harder and harder! I began to praise and shout and dance just like Karen. We were both in her living room praising God like we were in a church service. I couldn't believe my God had healed me right there in her living room!

I went home to show my family the miracle that had just happened to me. I ran in the house calling for my husband. He came yelling, "What's wrong." He thought that something bad had happened to me. I told him, "No, no, look at my thumb. I can move it and it doesn't hurt." He asked me. "What happened, what did you do?" I told him, "I went over to Karen's house and we prayed and praised God and He healed me!" He just stood there and looked at me. I wiggled it around and I told him, "You know God had to heal me because just a few minutes ago it was extremely painful!" and he said, "Well yea." I walked away shouting, telling the kids what the Lord had just done for me. I shared that testimony to everyone I encountered. God was truly making a believer out of me. Prayer and praise is powerful!!! God didn't allow me to go to the hospital for a reason! It was another lesson I had to learn. He wanted to get all of the glory that day and He did.

I also know, sometimes you do have to go to the hospital, because there was another incident after this one and I tried to do the same thing. I prayed and I praised God but He didn't choose to heal me miraculously like he did with the thumb. I had to go through surgery. God is God all by himself and He does what He wants to do, how He wants to do it. In all of my learning, I am learning to trust Him because He will always bring us through. It may not always be the same way each time, but He will bring us through. He is a trustworthy and faithful God!

On My Own Two Feet

We were all living on post now, Carol, Karen and myself. Carol and I were inseparable. We worshipped together, prayed together, witnessed, shopped and cried together. One day Carol called me with a bit of bad news. Her husband had just received orders to a new duty station. I felt like I was going to die. My good friend and spiritual mentor, Carol, was leaving me. She was the one that helped me to hold it together. During her final days we tried to spend as much time together as we could. For the most part, I tried not to think about it too much. It was very stressful and scary for me. I would wonder many days "What will I do without her here?" I would ask myself over and over again, "How am I going to make it?"

Finally the day had come. Carol moved out of their quarters into the guesthouse on post. During the process of packing and helping her husband clean, she was very busy. We hardly communicated at all. One evening she called me and told me they were going to be leaving the following morning and wanted me to come by and see them before they left. It was a sad drive to the guesthouse. I remember walking, what seemed like forever down the hall to get to her room. I knocked on the door and stood gazing up the walkway waiting for her to open the door. I didn't mind because I knew that it would be the last time that I would have to wait for her and that wasn't a good feeling. Remember, Carol was always late! I didn't care, because no matter how long I had to wait, she was a blessing to me. She was my friend, no matter how slow she was. When she finally opened the door she had a big grin on her face just like the first day I met her.

She welcomed me in and I walked in knowing this may possibly be the last time I ever saw her again.

We had a nice visit and I had a chance to say goodbye to the girls. We hugged each other numerous times before it was over. Finally, we thought I had better leave, it was after midnight and they had to get up early in the morning and hit the road. We said our good byes and we exchanged information to keep in touch. I walked out and she closed the door behind me. It was late or shall I say early in the morning and I was walking to my car alone. I was concerned about that, but more focused on the thought of my best friend leaving me here by myself.

Tears began to fill up in my eyes and I heard this small voice say to me, "Don't you cry." As the tears fell I said, "What am I going to do?" Again, the same still gentle voice said to me, "You are going to stand on your own two feet now!" I thought to myself,

"How in the world am I going to do that?" While at the same time, I found myself believing the words I had just heard, "You will stand on you own two feet now." I knew even if Carol was leaving me, God would never leave me! If He said I would make it, I believed I was going to make it! I will have God with me at all times. I was really learning to totally lean and trust in Him.

Carol and I kept in touch with each other for years, but as most long distance relationships go, eventually we lost contact with each other. I always believed someday we would speak again. Then the unthinkable happened.

One day my spirit led me to call Carol. I had not spoken to her for a long time. I found out she and her husband had gotten a divorce. I was saddened to hear that, but she told me she was okay and had met someone else. Because I always like to hear the story of how people met, I asked her, "Where did you meet him?" She told me, "In a bar." In total disbelief, I immediately asked her, "What were you doing in a club to meet this man?" That is when she began to tell me that she had started back sliding and that she wasn't as close to the Lord as she had been. As she talked, I became totally numb. I couldn't believe my ears! I was talking to myself as she was talking to me. I felt like screaming, I felt like crying, I felt like fussing at her. I didn't know what to think, feel or say. Then I asked her, "Why?" She had an explanation, but it didn't sit well with me. All I remember asking myself was, "How does this kind of thing happen to a person like her? Carol knew the word inside and out. She even knew some Greek and Hebrew language. She studied the Bible like nobody I ever knew." I was having a very difficult time comprehending what she was telling me. Then I became alarmed. All I could think was, "If this could happen to her, a lady who was as close to God as she was, what in the world was going to happen to me?"

We talked, I tried to witness to her and it seemed to fall on death ears. I don't remember why but we ended the conversation and I have no idea where she is or what she is doing. After talking to Carol, I decided to tighten up the reins. I didn't want to walk that close to the Lord and then turn and walk away. I continued to ask God what happened to Carol and prayed she would seek Him. I was sad, very sad in my soul. I was so afraid of possibly losing my salvation one day, and backsliding again!

I immediately made a decision that I wasn't going to let anything separate me from my God. Not mother, father, children, husband or anything was going to come between us. I figured that if I lost Him I would lose everything anyway, but if I kept God (Jesus) in my life, I would be able to hold onto what ever needed to be in my life. I knew that with Him "I could do all things through him who gives me strength," and "By myself I can do nothing." (Philippians 4:13 & John 5:30a)

Chapter 10 Warning!

While working at Jostens in Clarksville, Tennessee, I was feeling really down. On my first break I called my sister Sharmel in California and told her I couldn't take the abuse anymore. To call from work, things must have been awful. I was at my wits end and I wanted out. I told her what I was going through. She didn't ask many questions, but offered to get a U-haul and come and pick us up. Because she was at work, she had to put me on hold. I really needed to get back to work because my break was only for fifteen minutes. As I stood at the pay phone, I saw my reflection and heard a soft quiet voice say, "If you leave you will be sorry!" I said to myself, "Huh," and I heard it again but only louder, "IF YOU LEAVE YOU WILL BE SORRY!" It was with such authority until it put fear in me. It scared me so bad, by the time my sister got back on the phone, I told her, "That's okay, I don't need you to come and get me." She said, "I'm sorry for taking so long to get back on the phone, it's no problem, we can come and get you!" I said, "No, it's not that you took so long to get back on the phone, I changed my mind because God told me that I would be sorry if I left." I knew the life I had in California and I could only imagine what He meant by "being sorry." I dare not take the chance.

I couldn't afford to go against the word of the Lord. I didn't know exactly what would have happened to me if I left, but I did know one thing for sure, I didn't want to find out! I told her to hold off on coming and I would call her back later to explain. I really had to get back to work. That was the day I made a decision to go through what ever I had to go through and to stay in the will of God

It wasn't easy living this kind of life. Never knowing from day to day how I was going to be treated by my husband. Not knowing how I was going to respond. Having to take this abuse was new for me, but I was willing to learn how to handle it God's way. For so long I had done things my way and the results were not favorable. I knew that in order for me to have a successful life I had to do things God's way this time around. I referenced the scripture, Luke 11:25-26 New King James Version(NKJV)

"And when he comes, he finds it swept and put in order. Then he goes and takes with him seven other spirits more wicked than himself, and they enter and dwell there; and the last state of that man is worse than the first." I had no intentions on backsliding ever again. Just the thought of my life becoming worst than it was during my drug addiction days was enough to keep me pressing on!

Battle Field of the Mind

I had to learn how to live with mixed emotions. There were many days that I didn't want to be living the way I was living, mostly unhappy. I sat around and thought about everything that was going wrong in my life, but if I counted my blessings all day and kept my mind on happy thoughts, meditating on the things that were going good for me and my family, then I felt good about my life. I had a battle of the mind everyday. I had to fight just to feel good about the day. Many days I won the battle and some days I lost it.

I was glad to be together as a family again; I was overjoyed to be able to take care of my children myself, and be the mother I should have been all along. Even though we didn't have any material processions, we had each other. We were together as a family. It was sad being away from our immediate family, but God put some wonderful people in our lives and we appreciated everything that He was blessing us with.

There were many days, if I allowed my mind to wonder, I would get depressed. I had to learn how to shake it off, snap back and focus on the positive. For me it was truly a battlefield of the mind, but a battle I was determined to win!

Whenever we fought and argued, I always reverted back to, "Why did I come here, did I hear God correctly? Is it something that I am doing wrong? Was I worthy of anything else but misery!" There were many days the thought crossed my mind to give it all up, go back to what I was use to doing, because I was never going to amount to anything. I listened to the lies the enemy told me, only for a moment and then I listened to the word that would begin to come up in my spirit. I would hear words like, "No weapon formed against you shall prosper and every tongue which rises against you in judgment you shall condemn" Isaiah 54:17a NKJV, or "There is therefore now no condemnation to those who are in Christ Jesus, who do not walk according to the flesh, but according to the Spirit" Romans 8:1 NKJV. Every time I made a mistake the enemy would try and condemn me and bring up my past and the person that I used to be.

I had to speak the word back to him. I had to learn to speak the word and I had to do it quickly. It was the most critical part of my survival, but I didn't know it at the time. I stayed in the word and it was committed to my memory. Along with the help of my friend, Carol, who discipled me, because she always spoke the word of God to me. Very seldom did she offer her opinion alone.

Then one day it just began to spring up in me like a well. I learned the word of God is powerful (Hebrews 4:12 NKJV) "For the word of God is living and powerful, and sharper than any two-edged sword, piercing even to the division of soul and spirit, and of joints and marrow, and is a discerner of the thoughts and intents of the heart." I found out my mind had to be renewed and it was going to be washed by the word of God (Romans 12:2 NIV) "Do not conform to the pattern of this world, but be transformed by the renewing of your mind. Then you will be able to test and approve what God's will is—his good, pleasing and perfect will." I had to learn how to let the word of God change who I was. It wasn't easy, but because I was willing, I believe that is how the change came about. I had to die to self and take on the mind of Christ.

"Old things have passed away; behold, all things have become new" (2Corinthians 5:17b). I had to take the word of God and renew my mind, renew my way of thinking and renew my way of handling situations. My perception of things had to change. Everything about me had to change and it was going to be a process. The process was going to take place by reading God's word, praying, and DOING the will of God! It is really a humbling experience. I had become the type of person who felt they had to step up in order to protect myself and not allow people to run all over me. Learning to live life God's way often times made me fell like a chump.

I felt if I didn't say something or do something; others considered me a wimp. I didn't want to be classified that way only because I didn't want to be taken advantage of any more. My mind was all messed up. I was learning that it was okay to be meek. Some may say I'm not meek enough but compared to the person I used to be, I am very meek. Sometimes I amaze myself at the response that I give because I can surely remember the day when I wouldn't tolerate much. I have learned that silence really is golden.

For instance, the Bible says, "My dear brothers and sisters, take note of this; Everyone should be quick to listen, slow to speak and slow to become angry" (James 1:19 NIV). I used to be the exact opposite. I discovered I was so far from the way God intended for me to be. I had to change of my ways.

I was a runner. If I didn't like a situation, I got out of it. If it was a job, I would give my notice and leave. I had no problem finding new jobs so that wasn't an issue for me. I believe that's why I liked working for temporary agencies. I didn't have to stick around for long if I didn't like a job or the people. Not now though. I had to stay in this situation because the Lord said so. I wanted to leave and He told me if I left I would be sorry. I still could have left if I wanted to but I was warned. I really thanked God for the heads up (warning). Because of the warning, I took heed and I stayed. Many years ago on my current job, I wanted to leave for one reason or another, and I heard the Lord tell me to stay put. He told me that he was going to develop my character. I had to obey, even though many times I tried to talk myself into leaving.

Still Fighting in the Spirit!

Sometimes you have to run! Even though God was blessing my family, the enemy was still raging in our lives. As happy as I was for us to be living on post and in our new place, we still were having family problems. My husband was showing the manifestation of God and his loving, kindness towards us, yet he still chose to act deviant from time to time. When he drank he was at his worst, which was several days a week.

We had just moved into our new apartment in Pierce Village and my husband came home drunk. We still had keys to the old apartment in Lee Village. I was standing in the dining room cleaning and he was in my face cursing and calling me names. I stood there looking at him wondering what was wrong with him and what he was accusing me of this time. I was busy and I was tired. Tired from the work of the day and tired of him belittling me for no reason. We had plenty of work to do to clear the old house and get things straightened in this new house. He was standing with his back to the kitchen door. Leaning up against the wall was a baseball bat. All I can remember is while he was yelling at me I could hear a voice in my head saying, "Pick up the bat and hit him in his head." He kept yelling and I kept hearing this voice say, "Pick up the bat and hit him across the head, he is drunk so he probably won't be able to stop you!" I looked at the bat and I thought about it. I was tired of the abuse. He was yelling and I was looking at the bat seriously wanting to pick it up. I heard another voice say, "Run!" My adrenalin was rushing because I was becoming more hostile with him for cursing at me. He wouldn't stop! Why won't he stop and leave me alone? I looked at the bat again, and I heard this voice again say very loudly, "RUN!!!"

I took off running through the living room. I ran round the stairs and through the door that led to the garage. I ran out of the garage and down the street. I could hear him calling my name, "Sha, Sha, come back here. Where are you going?" I kept running faster and faster. I ran almost all the way to the other house in Lee Village on Dixie Road. I went inside, I ran upstairs and sat on the bedroom floor. All I could do was cry. I tried to slow down my breathing, not make so much noise and cry silently, but it was very difficult. My heart was beating rapidly and pounding against my chest as I sat on a empty bedroom floor in a pool of my tears.

I was angry because I couldn't hurt him the way he was hurting me. I was making the right choice and sometimes in doing so I got frustrated because

I wanted to handle things with my flesh! All I was doing was trying to be a good wife and help and all I got was abuse and slander. I was fed up with this kind of treatment.

I was sad for myself, and what I was going through, but I was glad that God saved me from a horrible situation. God knew I couldn't take very much more and that is why he told me to run. I believe had I not ran that day, something terrible would have happened. I would have lost my freedom that day. Thanks to God he saved my life and the life of my husband. After sitting there for a while and calming myself down, I had a little talk with the Lord.

It was getting dark and I felt it was safe for me to go back home. God had to really calmed me down. It's not that I wanted to hurt my husband, but I was going to do what I had to do to make him stop hurting me. I had to continue to pray and pray hard. I was really praying for my husband to get delivered from alcohol because it showed a bad side of him. He would be at his worst and always tell me that a drunk doesn't lie. That is what made it so bad.

He would say things when he was drunk and wouldn't remember them when he was sober. He wanted to talk when he was drunk and I wanted to talk to him when he was sober. I had to deal with all of this, take care of my two darling little children, and try to live a normal life. I had no family here and I only had a few friends, so I had to depend solely on the Lord to council me, comfort me and calm me down.

Saudi War

My husband came home from work and told us that it was his time to leave and go to war. I thought, “Oh my God!” It had finally come time for him to leave.

We did not know how to think or feel. We were sad and wanted to spend as much quality time together as we could. There were a lot of things we needed to get done before he left, such as legal matters. I was assigned power of attorney so I could take care of business in my husband’s absence. He was concerned I would do something that he wouldn’t approve of. I assured him I wouldn’t do such a thing. I knew with my track record he had to fight the bad thoughts of what could happen. It was a chance that he decided he would take. I told him he didn’t have to worry about anything and I really felt he didn’t. It was a gamble for him; especially since he wasn’t 100% sure I was delivered. I know he still had his doubts, but it was a chance that he was willing to take.

I had no intentions on doing anything with the power of attorney. It was comforting to know he was willing to trust me. I knew I had to win the confidence of everyone again. I knew I was changed, but they still needed some convincing. After all, it was easy to fall off of the wagon. Sometimes people go clean and sober for ten years or more and then relapse. I knew he would be thinking of this from time to time. It had only been about four years for me.

It was a very difficult time for the children, especially my son. My daughter was so young I don't think she really realized what was going, but my son was thirteen years old. It was stressful for him and he tried to give me a hard time. Our family wasn't the only one going through this. It affected many homes. People were panicking everywhere. Each day the news had something bad to report. I thought I was going to lose my mind.

My husband's best friend was deployed also. His wife Susan had two children as well. She recorded the news faithfully. I couldn't do that. I watched it occasionally. It was a very emotionally and difficult time. During my waking hours my mind went into the "What if mode." Many of my friends and neighbors were leaving and going home to be with relatives. They couldn't handle the pressure of being there alone. It felt like I couldn't stand the pressure either but I didn't want to uproot the children for a year or so and then bring them back. Some ladies found comfort in cheating on their husbands and others found solace in spending a lot of money. I decided to stay away from the news as much as possible. I spent a lot of time trying to keep my mind under control, which was very difficult for me.

For some reason, we always want to assume the worst. We have a tendency to allow our minds to run with false information. It is an imagination that is not conclusive and we will entertain that thought as if it was factual. As much as I knew I should not allow my self to do so, I would do it almost every day. After church one Sunday, a group of ladies were standing around talking and I walked up and joined them.

They were talking about news concerning the war they had just heard and it wasn't good. As they were talking they glanced over to me as if to say, "It may be your husband." Immediately I said, "Why?" then I just stopped and briskly walked away. I knew that if I opened my mouth it wouldn't be pleasant and I didn't want to do that in church. I couldn't understand why someone would do that when they didn't have any names or proof that it was true. I walked off and got my children and went home.

Mind over matter was the biggest challenge for me during this critical time. One day I was talking to one of my neighbors and she asked me how I could be so calm and I told her it wasn't that I was calm it is that I chose not to verbalize my thoughts because they were only assumptions. I told her that I was having a real difficult time holding on emotionally, but I was doing a lot of praying and I was trying to stay away from the news and remain positive, which was challenging. There were a lot of people I had to stay away from just because of that.

I had told myself that until they came and knocked on my door, my husband was coming home and that is what I chose to believe until situations or circumstances proved otherwise.

I couldn't allow myself to continue to wonder how I was going to survive as a widow when I might not become one. I had to choose to believe and hope for the best. She said, "Well I guess that is a good way to look at it." I told her it was the best way for me to try and handle what was going on around me. Every time she came down to my house she had a horror story to tell about the war and some gossip about what women were doing in the neighborhood. One of my neighbors asked me why I didn't like to come outside and talk with the ladies when they would gather in the back yard. I told her it wasn't that I was trying to be antisocial, but I didn't want to sit and talk about what they were talking about. I couldn't handle all of the negativity and doubt. **They didn't want to pray and believe and I didn't want to doubt and gossip.** It wasn't beneficial to me. It just made matters worst.

I was driving home from Clarksville and I didn't have the music on, which is uncommon for me. I believe I was in a very depressed mood that day. I was driving but I felt like I was in a daze. I was in the car but my mind wasn't on what I was doing. I remember thinking, 'What if I become a widow?" Again I thought, I am too young to be a widow. What would my children do if they lost their father, what if, what if?" My mind was going on and on and I couldn't control it. I wanted to break down and cry. Then I heard a voice say, "Turn on the music." I didn't want to turn the music on so I didn't. Then I heard it again, but I didn't move because I didn't want to hear any music, which was strange for me. I kept hearing it until finally I quickly reached forward and I pushed in a tape. It was playing but it was down so low I could hardly hear it. The spirit of the Lord said, "Turn up the music" of course I didn't want to, but I did.

Well how many of you know you can actually hear something but not pay any attention to it. We'll, that is what I was doing. The music was playing but I wasn't listening to it at all. Then the spirit of the Lord told me, "Listen to the music." Finally I thought I would listen. The Clark Sisters were singing this song, "Wonderful Counselor." The chorus says "He promised perfect peace to him whose mind is stayed on Him." Finally, I realized there was a message for me. I started the song over from the beginning, and REALLY listened. I knew it was the LORD trying to speak to me and give me an answer. Yes, yes, that is my answer, I kept rewinding and rewinding it and then I began to sing it. I could feel the depression lifting from me. I had to keep my mind on Christ in order to have peace. All I wanted was some peace in the midst of the storm, "Desert Storm." When I went home, I decided to look up the scripture because I knew it was in the Bible. That is why I liked to listen to the Clark Sisters because a lot of their songs were about the word of God. From that point on, all the way home I had a wonderful time. I looked up the scripture. I was so excited!

Isaiah 26:3 New King James Version (NKJV)

"You will keep him in perfect peace; Whose mind is stayed on You, because he trusts in You." After reading that scripture it became one of the many I used to help me make it during the very difficult time of war. I shared it with as many as I could. I was able to remain positive and I was learning to trust in God. If I believed God to bring my husband home safe then I need not to worry that he wasn't going to come home safe. I then realized that when I worried, I didn't concentrate, and by not concentrating I opened myself up (naturally and spiritually) to many things that could happen. I could be killed in a car crash worrying about him or injure someone else.

I decided to get busy to help keep myself occupied so I wouldn't have a lot of idle time on my hands. I read in the newspaper one day, the craft center on post was offering a free class on how to decorate sweat shirts. I decided to take the class because it might be good to help me pass the time away. I really got into it. I made so many shirts until people started wanting me to make shirts for them. What was supposed to be a hobby became a catalyst for me to make some extra money and God knew we could use the extra cash.

Finally, we got the news that my husband's unit was coming home. We were all very elated and relieved. "What should I wear, how should I comb my hair?" You talk about nervous. The process took so long until by the time he actually got off the plane the children were asleep and all of us were worn out. We had gone back and forth to the hanger all night. But finally our soldiers were home. I never will forget it. The next day was Easter Sunday (resurrection Sunday is what I liked to call it). I'm not one that likes to miss church, but I decided I wasn't going to go to church that day. I had bought the children new outfits for church, so they were going, but I was staying home with my husband.

That year we spent apart, seemed like forever. The reunion was sweet. We had a wonderful time. Until all hell broke loose again.

I would like to put this plug in right here because this book will probably come out during the War in Afghanistan. My heart goes out to all of the parents, wives, children and families of every soldier deployed. We can't pray enough for our soldiers. I am still employed at Fort Campbell, KY. I work closely with the children and some of the wives and husbands of the deployed. I do the same thing today as I did back when my husband was at war. I pray and believe for them to come home safe. To me, that is the most effective thing that I can do.

It is heart wrenching when we hear of casualties of war. It just tears my heart apart. We try to be understanding and remain prayerful for all who are affected by the war and casualties of war. Many of my friends and co-workers are still dealing with husbands and friends that are having side affects of the war in Desert Storm. So even if they do come home it does not stop there!

There is no doubt that tragedy is in the land and we as Christians can only hope and pray and believe for the best. We have to love and reach out in love to others, and be there for one another during these critical times. I realize there are a lot of women and men whose mates are at war and they don't know the Lord and I can only imagine what they must be going through. When I hear of some of the things going on, it does not surprise me, but I know the best thing I can do to help is pray for them. Prayer does change things and I pray that this war will soon be over and our men and woman can come home and be with their families once and for all. **"PRAYER" THIS IS OUR GREATEST WEAPON OF WAR!**

A lot took place while my husband was overseas. He didn't get the promotion like he was supposed to and after trying to fight it he decided he no longer wanted to be in the military. I prayed and I tried to talk him into staying. I prayed and I prayed. It really wasn't a good time to transition due to the economy. Jobs were scarce and everyone was advising us against it. The more I prayed it seemed like the more he was set on getting out. One day while I was praying I heard the Lord say to me, "Line up with him and come in agreement." So that's what I did. I found me a word in the Bible to stand on and it was Psalms 37:25 (NKJV) "I have been young, and now am old; Yet I have not seen the righteous forsaken, Nor his descendants begging bread." Also I found Matthew 18:19 (NKJV) "Again I say to you that if two of you agree on earth concerning anything that they ask, it will be done for them by My Father in heaven."

I knew what the Lord was saying. If I come in agreement with my husband and stand on his word everything was going to be all right for us. When I saw I couldn't change his mind and the Lord clearly spoke to me to line up with him, I got my assignment and I began to pray and speak the word of God everyday. I spoke it to everyone who tried to put doubt in my mind that we were not going to make it if he got out of the military. I remember saying to someone, "It didn't matter if no one had a job, I knew my husband was going to get a job because we were not going to be forsaken and we were not going to beg for bread." I expected God to honor his word.

The Military had some job fares on post and my husband went to them and he came home very discouraged. He didn't get hired on the spot. He knew he wanted to be a truck driver, which is something he did while he was in the military. He had all of the qualifications, but for some reason he didn't get hired. All he wanted to do was sleep. He was suffering from depression and he didn't want to go to work either. I had to do a lot of praying and I had to encourage him.

It was time for him to get out of the military, and we were moving off post and he still didn't have a job lined up. My son was in high school so we decided to stay in Kentucky instead of going back to California. We moved to Hopkinsville. We moved into a tiny apartment. It was so small we had to get a storage unit for some of our belongings. It was the best thing that we could find at the time. My husband was still depressed and I was still praying and getting a little nervous, I must admit. Because my husband didn't have a job, he went to apply for unemployment.

They gave him an appointment to come back and speak to someone. That wasn't comforting to him at all. God is awesome and, of course, he did come threw for us. Before my husband could go back to the unemployment office he got a call from a trucking company. They wanted him to start immediately. I Praised God like I didn't have any sense. I was so grateful and I told everyone in the house that they needed to give God some praise for what he had done. I tell you the truth, my husband has been driving trucks every since and it has been over 18 years. God is Faithful!

It is amazing to me that in five years we moved six times. We moved four times in the state of Kentucky. One of my determining factors (I thought) in coming here to be with my husband was, I thought I was going to travel and see the world. My husband always got orders to PCS (permanent change of stations) but they were always deleted. A lot of my friends got to go to Germany and different places, but I didn't get to go anywhere. I never understood why. I guess it wasn't meant to be.

After living in that tiny apartment for a short period of time, we decided to buy a house. The whole process was more difficult than I thought. My husband was on the road most of the time. I had to do most of the work by myself. He told me the type of house he was looking for and it was my job to go and find it. I looked everywhere. Finally, I found one that fit the description I thought. I can't remember exactly what all of the terms were but I had to sign for the house so it wouldn't get away. I told my husband about the house and he was excited and he couldn't wait to get home and see it. The house had a basement, a swimming pool and it was in Tennessee. It was on a cul-de-sac and in a wooded area. I just knew he would love the house.

When he came off of the road, the realtor agreed to meet us at the house. During the whole walk through, my husband appeared to like the house. So when we finished looking at it the realtor asked him what he thought about the house. He told her, "It's nice can we call you later and talk about it?" She said, "Sure that will be fine." As soon as my husband closed the door to the car he looked at me and said, "I don't know what you're going to do to get us out of this house, but you better do something because I don't like it!" I said, "Why did you tell them you liked the house?" And he said, "I didn't want to say No, I don't like the house! I know one thing you better get us out of that house!" I told him, "I already signed for the house and there is nothing that we can do" He said, "You better do something!" I was so upset I didn't know what to do. That is why I hated handling business affairs because something would always go wrong and then it would be my fault.

I did what I knew how to do best. I went crying and praying to the Lord to please help me get myself out of this mess. I cried and I prayed, "Please help me Lord get out of buying this house!" I decided to call the realtor and tell her what was going on. Even she was in shock. She asked me, "I thought your husband liked the house?" I told her, "I did too, but when we got in the car, he told me what he didn't like about the house and that I had better get him out of the deal." Mrs. Realtor assured me that there wasn't anything she could do and we were locked in the deal. I acted like I didn't even hear her and I kept praying to God for help.

Late the next night I got a call from the realtor and she told me a bill was just passed and that if I didn't want to buy the house I would be able to get out of the deal. I didn't care what bill she was talking about, I was just glad to get the news. That whole situation was about to make me sick. I was so relieved to tell my husband the good news and I also let him know that the next house we would be considering to buy would be the one he found. I was finished with looking for houses and I meant just that. I had enough!

The realtor called me after a few days and she asked me if I wanted to go looking for more houses and I told her I was done with looking and that my husband was going to find the house himself. She said, "Okay, but if there is anything I can do for you just give me a call." I said, "Okay" and I hung up in relief. I meant what I said; I had had enough of looking around trying to figure out what it was that he was really looking for. He only came home every two weeks so it was taking us a while to find a house. One day the realtor called me and said we needed to have a house built. I told my husband she was suggesting we build a house and he liked the idea. To make a long story short, we agreed to do that.

I was excited and I was looking at all kinds of books to gather ideas for the type of house to build. The house we were having built really should have not been classified as a build to suit, because it was actually a tract home. They already had in mind what kind of house they were going to build and we could only choose from the few that they had. If we altered the floor plan the price was outrageous. There were a lot of things that I was told that were going to happen that didn't and it made me very angry. I had a hard time forgiving the realtor and the builder for what they had done to us. I had to pray long and hard to forgive all involved for lying and deceiving us. For the most part, we were not satisfied but we made do.

Forgiveness

I told this story because I didn't want to behave like a non-Christian during this ordeal. I was really upset and I wanted to hurt somebody. I knew I couldn't do that so I decided to file a lawsuit. I soon realized it was going to be a long process. I had to let it go. It was very hard for me to do and every time I thought I had forgiven the realtor I would see a car that resembled hers and I could literally feel something rise in me and I knew I had not forgiven her. I had to go back in prayer and try to let it go again. I must admit it took much prayer to finally, truly forgive the realtor. When I did, we became friends again and I enjoyed her company until she left the area.

Every time I would go and visit at her home, she felt the need to give me something; as to make up for my disappointment I guess. I tried to tell her for me it was a thing of the past and I held no grudge against her. But I understood where she was coming from because people have a tendency to say a lot of things that they really don't mean.

What she didn't realize, I had truly forgiven her and I had put it all behind me. I tell this story because sometimes we will find ourselves in a position where we have truly been wronged and the Lord will instruct us to forgive and let it go. In our mind we feel we have the right to retaliate but God may say let it go, and forgive, and it will benefit you to do just that. It may not be easy, but it is possible and beneficial. It would also be detrimental to you if you don't. **Forgiveness is so Powerful! Unforgiveness is deadly!**

If we do not forgive then we should not expect God to forgive us because he will not! Matthew 6:14-15 (NIV) "For if you forgive other people when they sin against you, your heavenly Father will also forgive you. But if you do not forgive others of their sins, your Father will not forgive your sins."

We had some wonderful times in that house. Although we no longer live in the house, we still own it and it is a blessing to us and to others. I learned a valuable lesson and I have to carry it with me everyday. I can't expect God to forgive me when I have unforgiveness towards others in my heart. I had to learn to let it go. Every day, by the end of the day, we should let go of anything that we have against others. The word of God speaks of it in Ephesians 4:26 New King James Version (NKJV)"Be angry, and do not sin": do not let the sun go down on your wrath." I had to realize that.

What I was doing was trying to cover myself under the blood by making sure my sins were forgiven, but then I would get right up from praying and harbor unforgiveness in my heart towards others. In Christ it does not work that way. When I read the scripture in the Bible, I was in awe. I couldn't believe I had been so wrong and that in order for me to be right I had to do the right thing. We can't say we love God and treat His people any kind of way. It just doesn't work like that.

Life was going good for us for a change. Even though my husband was gone most of the time, he was fulfilling his life long dream. I didn't want him to be on the road and gone so much but I didn't want to crush his dreams either. I have had so many of my dreams crushed and stolen from me, until I couldn't do that to him. If being a truck driver is what he wanted to do, then by all means go and do it. I stayed home with the children. God was blessing me on my job and in my Church. I would get to go back home to California for the entire summer and I was content with that.

Chapter 18 Holy, Holy, Holy

I started a women's ministry called the "Daughters of Destiny." It is an awesome ministry, I was now singing on the praise team and I was part of the jail ministry. I became a part of the praise team because one day in prayer the Lord told me I was going to sing. I was surprised and I said nothing to any one. I really do love to sing. I have been singing all of my life. My voice is nothing like it was when I was younger thou.

God had blessed me with a beautiful voice and I almost destroyed it completely. I thank God for what I have left. I pray constantly for total restoration. The constant use of drugs and alcohol almost totally destroyed my voice. Nonetheless, I still love to sing and praise the Lord. I love music!

When He spoke those words to me I was excited. I figured that if He said I was going to sing, He was going to open the door for me to walk in. When I went to church they made an announcement; if any body wanted to sing on the praise team to stay after church. I almost screamed. This was my opportunity. I went and talked to the praise leader after church and she said, "Yes."

To this day, I am still singing on that same praise team. Since I have come to Christ and He knows I love music, He fixed it and now I am using my gift in the right place.

I used to love to go out and party but I have come to find that there is no party like a Holy Ghost Party because a Holy Ghost Party doesn't stop. That is a saying we have in the church. You have never really been drunk until you get drunk in the spirit. There is not a day that goes by that I miss dancing in the club because I now do the dance in the Church for the Lord as a form of praise. After all, I was created to praise the Lord not the devil and I will never take my dance to his house ever again.

A lady in the church started a jail ministry and she came up with her team and they would go and minister to the ladies in the jail twice a month. It was something that I really desired to do, but I felt that if God wanted me to do it, he would open the door for me to go. I never said anything to anyone about it. One day the lady that started the ministry had to leave because her husband came down on orders. She put Mrs. Pam in charge of the ministry and replacing for her. I heard about it and I really did want to say something but I didn't.

My sister heard about the opening and she asked me if I was going to inquire about the position. I told her I was going to tell God about it and leave it alone. When I went to church one Sunday, Ms. P told me she had prayed about the replacement, and the Lord told her I was the one she was to choose. I said all of that to say, there are some things I just will not try and make happen for myself because I feel if God doesn't want me to be there then I don't need to put myself there.

Fell Out of Love with My Husband

While my husband was gone most of the time on the road, I was very busy with the house, children, church and my ministries. I was busy and I was growing in the Lord. I also felt I was growing apart from my husband.

It had gotten to the point when he came home I wasn't excited anymore. I was always busy and it seemed he wasn't into what I was into, and I wasn't into what he was into. I would think sometimes, "Why doesn't he just have an affair or something and then that way I will have a way out of this marriage." I knew according to the Bible if he committed adultery I would have the right to divorce him, if I elected to. I really wanted a husband I could pray with and we would enjoy reading the word together and go to church and praise God together. It wasn't happening that way for me and I was getting tired of praying the same prayers for him and there was no significant change. I thought it wasn't right for him to be here taking care of me and I really didn't care for him. So I began to tell the Lord in prayer how I was feeling. I had a long talk with God about how he needed to change and how he needed to get his life together. God really let me have it that day. I guess He had enough of my complaining. I had become so full of myself until I needed to be set straight before something terrible happened to me. I thank God for His rod of correction.

Rod of Correction

God politely spoke to me, "How dare you have that attitude towards your husband. How long did people have to wait for you to get yourself together? How long did people have to put up with you and your ways and drug addiction? How long?" All I could do at that point was cry and repent. I told God I was so sorry and I repented for being so high minded. God then spoke to me, He was going to deal with him but it was going to be at his timing and not at mine. My husband was going to have his own testimony just like I had mine. The very thing I didn't like people to do to me when I was trying to get myself together, I was now doing to my husband. Oh how soon we do forget! Then the Lord told me, "He has not changed, and he is the same person you fell in love with. It is not him, it is you!" I began to cry again. I cried out, "Oh my God, please help me, I don't want to be like this. Lord please help me fall back in love with my husband because I don't love him anymore." I mean I lay there and I cried out to God in desperation because I knew I had gotten off the mark. I had grown up a little in the Lord and I had lost my love and compassion for my husband. I had become haughty in spirit.

It didn't take God long at all. It was as if God was just waiting for me to confess it and He was ready to release my deliverance. When my husband came home just a few days later, I was so excited to see him. I ran out of the house and into his arms. He looked at me like, what is wrong with you? What have you done or what do you want is the look he was giving me. He was also smiling, so I know that it made his heart glad.

The Lord had even spoken to me concerning my appearance. He told me to have my hair and nails done by the time he arrived home. Before when he came home it seemed as if I always would be in the middle of doing my hair and it would be standing up all over my head. When he came home that day I was ready. When I looked at my husband he actually looked different to me. He was the same, I just saw him differently...I realized it was a set up to cause us to break up. It also taught me to always examine myself to see if the problem is I, and not to always put the blame on the other person involved. Just another example of why prayer is so important. In prayer is where I found the answer to the problem.

When we held each other in our arms, I felt something on the inside I had not felt in a while. I actually was a little nervous like I had just met him, like he was my first love. I thank God for correcting me that day because if He had not, I do believe I would have allowed some other spirit to enter in and I wouldn't be here with my husband today.

There were many times I would go to the Lord complaining about my husband and He wouldn't say a word to me about him. He would only talk to me about me! One time when I went to the Lord about something my husband was or wasn't doing the Lord told me that my husband was getting an "A" and I was failing. I asked him what He meant. He told me as a sinner he was doing and acting just like a sinner should. As for me, a Christian, I was failing because I wasn't being very Christ like. I wasn't exercising any of the fruit of the spirit at all when it came to my husband or my family for that matter.

One night when I came home from ministering at the jail, my husband and I got into it over something trivial. Later that night the Lord began to minister to me. He said, "Charity begins at home and then it goes abroad. The same care and under-standing that you are you giving to the women at the jail, you need to be exercising here at the house." After I meditated on what the Lord had spoken to me, I had to take a long hard look at myself and the way I was treating my family compared to how I was treating others on the outside of my home.

After carefully evaluating the situation, I found I was being more understanding and kind to others and God wasn't pleased with me. The Lord told me that He wasn't impressed with me at all and for the Lord to tell me something like that broke my heart. I called myself being a good steward and servant of the Lord, but I found out I was quite the contrary. Immediately I had to pray for myself and get it together and realize when dealing with my family, it is still ministry. They are to be treated gentle and kind just like we do people outside of our homes.

Praise I Couldn't Accept

At one of my Daughters of Destiny conferences, this lady came up to me and she was praising me for what I was doing with the women's ministry and how God was using me etc. This wasn't the first time someone had done something like this before, but it was the first time I responded like this. Usually when people thank me I say, "Thank God because He is the one that truly deserves the praise, not me." When the lady was standing there praising me, I felt as if I couldn't accept the praise, that what she was saying about me wasn't true. I knew how I was when I wasn't at the conference or at home or how I would blast someone if they didn't do what

I thought they should do the way I thought they should do it. I was severely disturbed in my spirit for the rest of the day.

For the entire conference I couldn't get that feeling out of my mind. When the conference was over, and by the way we had a wonderful blessed time in the Lord, I had to go into prayer about the whole situation. All I did was come right out and tell Him, "Lord I can't accept the compliments the lady was trying to give me." I said, "I need to know what you are saying about me. Lord will you please show me how you see me." Boy what did I say that for! As I lay there He began to speak to me and He went on and on until I told Him, "Okay, that is enough." But He didn't stop, He kept on talking and I began to weep. I wept and I repented because I didn't want to be displeasing to the Lord. I learned that day it does not matter what you or others think or feel about you. It only matters what God has to say. If it is not pleasing to God then it is not okay. It doesn't matter how many praise reports you get.

I knew from that day forward I had to always ask God to show me "me," through his eyes. I want Him to always search my heart and show me if there is anything in me that should not be there. I ask God to put a finger on me the minute that I do, say, think, or feel anything that is not pleasing to Him; and He does just that. I always ask God to search my heart, give me a clean heart and renew a right spirit in me.

Psalm 51:10(KJV) Create In me a clean heart, O God; and renew a right spirit within me.

While we are on this journey, it does not matter what we are doing for the Lord as much as it matters how we are doing it. If what we are doing is not done in love, then we are doing nothing. It means nothing to the Lord. Here are some scriptures to support what I am saying:

1 Corinthians 13:1-3 New International Version (NIV) If I speak in the tongues of men or of angels, but do not have love, I am only a resounding gong or a clanging cymbal. If I have the gift of prophecy and can fathom all mysteries and all knowledge, and if I have a faith that can move mountains, but do not have love, I am nothing. If I give all I possess to the poor and give over my body to hardship that I may boast, but do not have love, I gain nothing.

How do we know if we are walking in Love or not? We can see if we line up with the word of God. In 1Corinthians 13:4-8a(NIV) "Love is patient, love is kind. It does not envy, it does not boast, it is not proud. It does not dishonor others, it is not self-seeking, it is not easily angered, it keeps no record of wrongs. Love does not delight in evil but rejoices with the truth. It always protects, always trusts, always hopes, always perseveres. Love never fails!"

There you have it! God has made it very plain for us to see what love is and what it does. In all that I do I have to make sure that it is done in love. There is another scripture that I love. It was adopted for the Daughters of Destiny and also the Church. We say it after every service, and that is:

Psalm 19:14 New King James Version(NKJV)

"Let the words of my mouth and the meditation of my heart Be acceptable in Your sight, O LORD, my strength and my Redeemer."

Don't Become Overwhelmed

I know that it may seem like a lot to take in at one time, but in the word of God we are advised to work out our own salvation. Meaning God will work with us and all we have to do is cooperate and work with Him. Whatever He brings up in your life, that is what He wants to deal with you about at that time. The key is to keep the lines of communication open. We must communicate with Him throughout every day. Prayer is just talking to Him and staying in His presence long enough to allow Him to talk back to you. After prayer you will find he will continue to speak to you through out the day.

Find a Church Home

It is necessary to be faithful to a local Church so you can be taught the word of God. The Bible says in 2Timothy 2:15 King James Version King James Version (KJV)

"Study to show thyself approved unto God, a workman that needeth not to be ashamed, rightly dividing the word of truth."

The Bible also says in Hebrews 10:25 King James Version (KJV)

"Not forsaking the assembling of ourselves together, as the manner of some is; but exhorting one another: and so much the more, as ye see the day approaching."

I want you to know that all people don't grow at the same speed. Just like the trees. Some grow tall fast while others grow slow. Our job is just to love and pray that all keep growing and not fall by the way side. That is why I love the jail ministry!

I found so many women there that were just like me. They love the Lord, but they have a hard time making the connection. I believe God has me there so I can help them put all of this in perspective. I try to help them get a good understanding of what is going wrong in their life. Proverbs 4:7 New King James Version (NKJV)

"Wisdom is the principal thing; Therefore get wisdom. And in all your getting, get understanding."

Like myself, I had to understand and rightly divide the word of God, so I could effectively apply it to my life. God is using others and me across the nation in many ways to help people see the Light. I know many people know the word of God just like I did. I even had committed it to memory. But it wasn't until I learned how to effectively apply the word of God to my life that it worked for me!

Ephesians 1:17-19 New King James Version (NKJV)

"that the God of our Lord Jesus Christ, the Father of glory, may give to you the spirit of wisdom and revelation in the knowledge of Him, the eyes of your understanding [being enlightened; that you may know what is the hope of His calling, what are the riches of the glory of His inheritance in the saints, and what is the exceeding greatness of His power toward us who believe, according to the working of His mighty power."

John 1:1-5New King James Version (NKJV)

"In the beginning was the Word, and the Word was with God, and the Word was God. He was in the beginning with God. All things were made through Him, and without Him nothing was made that was made. In Him was life, and the life was the light of men. And the light shines in the darkness, and the darkness didn't comprehend[a] it.

John 8:12New King James Version (NKJV)

"Then Jesus spoke to them again, saying, "I am the light of the world. He who follows me shall not walk in darkness, but have the light of life."

God's Word is Powerful!

Hebrews 4:12 New King James Version (NKJV)

"For the word of God is living and powerful, and sharper than any two-edged sword, piercing even to the division of soul and spirit, and of joints and marrow, and is a discerner of the thoughts and intents of the heart."

I know now that the word of God will free me from anything. I am not going to try and preach because I am not a preacher, but I wrote my story to tell the world that I have proof that it works because it worked for me. The word of God is true. God is who He says He is and He will do what He says He will do. I have no doubt in my mind anymore. If I had to go the route that I did, to become a true believer, then so be it!

Chapter 19: Walking in Deliverance

I have come a long way in the Lord and one thing I can truly say; I have learned how to lean on the Lord. I have learned and am still learning to trust in Him and take Him at His word. I have learned to depend on Him. I don't put too much trust in man anymore but I do put trust in the Lord. What I do and the way I am on Sunday is the same way I am seven days a week. I don't turn on my religion and turn it off. Actually, I don't have religion, I have salvation and I walk in deliverance.

I had to realize after I got saved, I had many, many things I needed to be delivered from. And to be honest, I am still working on myself. Procrastination is on the chopping block now. I must get the victory over this thing! By faith I can truly say I will!

In 1989, Karen wanted me to go with her to visit a church in Hopkinsville called Holiness Church of

Deliverance. I really enjoyed myself that night. I went back on several occasions when they had special meetings. One day, in prayer, the Lord told me he wanted me to leave Assembly of God and join that ministry. God knew what I needed, and I am still a member.

Isn't that something! God made sure I got a good understanding of what I needed by putting me in a deliverance ministry. Since the first day I started going there I have learned so much about the word of God and myself. It has not always been easy to stay, and yes, there have been numerous times I have wanted and contemplated leaving for various reasons. But, I believe if this is where the Lord has placed me, then I'm not going to leave until He tells me to do so. I knew if I left, it would be me wanting to run again. If the lord doesn't say so then stay and get your goods. I have to stay where God has placed me and continue to work out my soul salvation. I have even prayed for permission to leave and it wasn't granted. I am to remain until He says otherwise and no one else. That is what I have done. I have stayed put.

A deliverance ministry is not an easy ministry to be in. At times, it is painful just like childbirth. There were days I felt like running as fast as I could to get away, but I knew better. Almost always when I felt like that, it was when the Lord was taking me higher in Him. To take on more of the Lord, meant shedding off more of me. To die to self is painful, and to be honest most of us don't like the pain that growth brings. Rather than to stay there and put up with the pain and grow, it seemed more natural to run and stop the pain. But it wasn't God's will for my life and I can truly say I am so glad I listened to the Lord and I didn't run!

Why?

Many might ask, "Why in the world would you write a book telling all of your business?" I decided to write the book because one day in 2003, I heard the Lord tell me I was going to write a book. Therefore, this book was written out of obedience. When I think about it now though, I started to write a book about my life when I was just a little girl but I never finished it. Even as a young girl, I had experienced so much, I felt the need to tell it, but it wasn't the time. I only completed a few pages. I didn't know that the book I was feeling on the inside of me to write then, was going to manifest itself some forty years later. Isn't that incredible?

The time for the book to go to the nations is now! For such a time as this! I know the enemy wants me to be ashamed of all of the things that I have done, but I don't look at it as telling on myself, because I know what I am doing is EXPOSING THE ENEMY AND GLORIFYING GOD! If telling my story and exposing the things I allowed the enemy to do to me and through me will save someone else's life or marriage, then I can't help but tell it. My life is a testimony of the awesome wonder working power of the one and only true and living God. It is also a testimony of what living a life of sin, and disobeying God will ultimately do to you!

It Wasn't Me

What I did is not the person I am. When I think about what I used to do, I have to shake my head in disgust and disbelief. If I didn't know I really did some of those things, I wouldn't believe it myself. Because of who I am today, it is hard to believe I used to be that way. I know I am not crazy and I know how sin and evil spirits work. I know first hand the things that the forces of darkness will make you do. It is as if you literally become someone else. I am a new person since I walked out of darkness and into the light. Old things have past away. It wasn't me; it was the spirits driving me.

2 Corinthians 5:17 New King James Version (NKJV) "Therefore, if anyone is in Christ, he is a new creation; old things have passed away; behold all things have become new."

I heard a story on the gospel channel about a man who had gotten locked up for some type of repeated sexual abuse of a minor and he was saying, he had given his life to the Lord and he was so glad to be free. He said I may be locked up in this prison for the rest of my life, but at least I am free. He said when he had his freedom, meaning not incarcerated, he was actually bound.

Booty Call

One day praying for the title of the book I heard "Booty Call, a call to Booty." "Lord am I hearing you correctly? Is this you or is this me?" I asked myself. When I stand here today and I take a look back over my life, I can clearly see God had a great plan for me. The enemy knew it, so he had to make sure he got me off course. There were many nights when I made a booty call. This little girl who had decided to live as a virgin until her husband came to get her was actually making booty calls as if there wasn't anything wrong with it.

It took me quite some time to realize that there was a "call to the Booty," but I had responded to the wrong one for a long, long time. What ever good God is doing, the enemy tries to counterfeit it.

The word **Booty** means: SPOIL TAKEN FROM AN ENEMY IN WAR; PLUNDER; PILLAGE; ANY PRIZE OR GAIN. Plainly put spoils of war, goods, treasure, valuables, livestock, etc. There was a war going on and I was called to get my goods! (Reference: Numbers 31: 1-54)

I can recall one night; I had finally fallen asleep, and had a dream. In the dream I was standing in this very dark place. There wasn't anything around me except for total darkness. On one side of me was this dark figure that was hurting me as it was pulling me towards it. On the other side of me was this figure in a white colored garment and it was pulling me towards it. They both had me by the wrist. The one on the dark side would snatch and pull me to its side and then the one with the white garment on would pull me back to the other side. There I stood in the middle being pulled from one side to the other. This went on for a while until suddenly I woke up in a panic.

I was so glad to be alive and I knew then that there was a war going on for my life. I knew the devil was trying to get me, but Jesus wasn't willing to let me go. I am so glad He didn't. When I woke up from the dream, I still couldn't bring myself to stop living this horrible life of sin. I wanted so much to live right for the Lord, but I just couldn't seem to get myself together and make it happen. Jesus was calling me to come with him and get the "booty."

I had been robbed of my goods and Jesus has called me to get my goods back. That war is over and I won with the help of the good Lord and I get the BOOTY! It was time for me to get my salvation back! It was time for me to get my joy back! It was time for me to get my peace back! It was time for me to get my children back! It was time for me to get my husband back and pray him through because God was concerned about his soul. It was time for me to get my dignity back! It was time for me to get my sanity back! It was time for me to get my praise back! It is time for you to get your Booty. God has your goods and He wants to get them to you.

It was an awesome thing the Lord showed me one day. From 1977 to 1987, ten years, I was lost on the street, acting like I was out of my mind. I had just graduated from high school; got married; had a baby; and a marriage split up, because I didn't know how to use my weapons of warfare. I had been in church all my life, I knew the word of God and I could sing all the songs, but I couldn't fight and save my marriage or keep my salvation. I let the enemy walk right into my life, my home and almost destroy us all. Oh, but God!

In 1987 I came back to Kentucky for what I thought was another summer vacation with the children, and it turned out to be God mending our family back together again. Only this time we had a new addition to the family that was obtained in an adulterous affair. My little miracle baby, Grace!

One day God showed me something. He told me it was the same set up as ten years earlier. In 1977 I gave in and became like everyone around me instead of standing my grounds. I didn't know how, or should I say, I just didn't choose to fight in the spirit and keep my salvation, my family or my marriage. By doing so, I lost everything and became the worst out of all.

Now fast forward 10 years to 1987 and I am a woman trying to live for the Lord, married to a man who wants nothing to do with the Lord or the church.

I was trying to be a good Christian wife and raise not one child but two. Most of our friends were my husband's and none of them were saved and they all liked to do the same things: party, drink and have fun. I didn't know anyone in Kentucky except the Lord, my husband and two children. I knew if I was going to make it, I had to get a hold of God like never before. God told me it was the same set up, and the only difference this time, He was going to show me how to fight and win. It wasn't easy, but in 2012, I can truly say I have won the war and I am going to continue to try and win every battle.

God has truly taught me how to fight and how to stand and I dedicate my life to telling others to hold on and don't let the enemy steal anything from them that the Lord wants them to have. My husband is saved and still growing in the Lord. My children are saved and now we are working on our grandchildren. God has been faithful to me down through the years and generations just like He promised He would. I know my grandchildren will be blessed also. I know my parents and siblings give God the glory for my salvation.

God is really real and He is in the deliverance business. I believe and know the blood of the lamb can set all of God's children free. I know because it happened to me. When I think about the things I used to do, I can hardly believe it! When I tell others about my past, they can't believe it either. I let them know, “That is just how good God is at cleaning us up, He leaves no residue!”

There is power in the name of Jesus. God sent his only begotten son, Jesus, to be the light of the World. We as Christians are to let our light shine like the Bible says in:

Matthew 5:16 New King James Version (NKJV)

“Let your light so shine before men, that they may see your good works and glorify your Father in heaven.”

This little light of mine, I am going to let it shine, and if telling of his awesome delivering power is shining light on Him, then I am going to do it. I will shout it from the mountaintop if someone wants me to. I believe there is a need for this to be known because Jesus really is real and people clearly need a Savior. Sin is running rampant through our land. So many people are addicted to drugs, alcohol, pornography, etc., which leads to other things that ultimately ruin their lives or the lives of others.

I am spreading the word that we don’t have to pretend any longer. Jesus knows all of our faults and all of our sins that have us bound. If you are not right then you can go to the father and confess your wrongdoing and He will help you make it right. I know we want man to think we have it all together. If we have a problem, we have the Lord who understands our weaknesses. If you are not a Christian He understands and He wants so much to help you to live a life free from sin.

Jesus said in his word in: Luke 19:10 New King James Version (NKJV) "For the Son of Man have come to seek and to save that which was lost." Jesus really does love his little children!

Power in the Name Of Jesus

I remember one night I had some money and I was walking up Adams Boulevard to a friend's house to buy some cocaine and get high. I was just a few feet away from his street and he lived a couple houses away from Adams. I didn't have far to go at all. A man pulled up to the curb and waited for me to walk by and then he let his power window down and called to me. I had no plans on stopping because I already had money and I wanted to go and start getting high. When I looked at him, he looked liked one of my mother's customers from the laundromat. I walked up to the car window and started talking to him. He asked, "Do you need a ride?" "No, I'm just going right around the corner," I said. He said, "Oh, come on and get in and I will take you." Well it seemed senseless to me because I only had a few feet to go, but I got in because he insisted. I told him to turn at the corner and pull over to the curb because the house was right there. He said, "Okay." When he pulled over to the curb, I told him, "Thank you" and I reached for the doorknob to get out. Suddenly, he sped off from the curb. Immediately, I turned my head back to ask him what he was doing.

To my amazement, when I looked at him this time, he looked like a different man. I realized I didn't know him.

It was as if he had changed his face. I am not kidding you! I was so scared. I began to scream and tell him to stop and let me out. I grabbed for the doorknob again and I heard him hit the power lock. I couldn't get the door open. I began to scream all the more. All I could think was, "Am I going to die tonight, will I ever see my children again?" Then I thought if he did something to me, I wasn't going to be able to get high either. He might take my money, then I will have to go and make some more. I was screaming and screaming to the top of my lungs. He then swung the car around the corner, and as I am still screaming and snatching on the door, he reached into his coat pocket and pulled out a knife and started yelling, "Shut up or I'm gonna stab you." Now I am really scared. I didn't want to die in this man's car or in the street somewhere and my children never see me again!

All of a sudden, I hear this quiet voice in my head say, "There's power in the name of Jesus," and again, "There's power in the Name of Jesus." I said to myself, "That is true" so I began to scream, "JESUS! OH GOD, OH JESUS, JESUS!!

I guess he didn't like me screaming Jesus so he began telling me, "Shut up, shut up before I hurt you." But I heard the voice again say; "There's power in the name of Jesus!" So I kept on screaming,

"JESUS!" louder and louder. He swung around another corner violently. As I screamed "JESUS!" the car door flew open. I looked at the door as if to say, "How in the world did you get open? You were just locked?" Then I turned and looked at the man and he was still yelling and waving this knife at me. I heard a voice in my head say, "Jump!" I looked out of the car at the road, scared to death to jump. I felt something lightly push me and I leaned over and fell out of the car. The back tire rolled over my foot. It was horrible and it hurt something terrible. I thought I had died and gone to hell because everything was so dark. The night was dark and the road was dark and I had my eyes closed tight.

Finally, when I came to what seemed to be a stop from hitting the ground, I opened my eyes and all I could see was red brake lights. I realized I wasn't dead. I said, "He's probably going to back up and come and get me." I told myself to jump up and run before he comes. It wasn't until I took the first step that I realized how hurt I really was. I tried to run, one of my legs was going back further than normal, my foot hurt like it had been cut in half and my whole right side was in excruciating pain. I didn't give up. I couldn't run like I was used to, but I knew I had to keep moving. I hopped and limped out of the street and through people's yards. I found somewhere to hide for a minute because I didn't want him to catch me and I was in no condition to run.

I hid for a while because he was riding around looking for me. When I didn't see him anymore, I decided to try and creep home and get in the house. I had to walk all the way up Adams Boulevard to Labrea Boulevard, which was about ten blocks. I walked, looked and cried. My leg and foot hurt me so bad. I couldn't believe this had just happened to me. About five doors from my mother's house, I began to think. I am going to have to go to the doctor because something was definitely wrong with me. I decided to turn around and go to another friend's house and get high so when I went to the doctor, I wouldn't be able to feel the pain.

I had to turn around and walk several more blocks. When I got there his wife answered the door. I assumed she had just woke up because it was early in the morning and she still had on her gown. I bought the cocaine from her and we both sat there and smoked. Her husband came in the room and I had to get up for something. He noticed I was bleeding and he asked me what happened. When I told him, he cursed me out and told me to get my things together because he was going to take me to my mom's house because I needed to go to the hospital.

When we arrived he actually walked me to the door and rang the doorbell. When my mother finally opened the door he said, "Ma'am I brought your daughter home because she is hurt and needs to go to the hospital!" Mom opened the door, and looked at me with fear in her eyes. As she attempted to help me to the couch, she grabbed me and began to cry like I never heard her cry before. The sound of her cry in my ear broke my heart and made me cry. It was a cry of such pain it seemed tangible. So as we sat on the couch, we both cried together.

Someone called my soon-to-be brother-in-law and he came over and took me to the hospital. I had to have crutches because my foot was severely bruised. I also had a huge scar on my right thigh where several layers of skin had been scraped off by the asphalt. At the time, I couldn't help wondering if I was going to lose my foot. I had to and stay off of it for a while. I still have the scar on my thigh to this day. It serves as a reminder!

I know that Jesus rescued me that night. He didn't spare me all of the agony and pain I had to endure but He did spare my life. I know it was the power of "The Name of Jesus" that made that locked car door swing open so I could get out.

The forces of darkness had me seeing things. I knew I recognized the driver of that car, but when he wouldn't let me out, I saw him for who he really was. He was a stranger to me. From that day until now, I know and believe there is power in the name of Jesus.

The Truth Shall Make You Free

John 8:31-36 New King James Version (NKJV)

"Then Jesus said to those Jews who believed Him, "If you abide in My word, you are My disciples indeed. And you shall know the truth, and the truth shall make you free."

They answered Him, "We are Abraham's descendants, and have never been in bondage to anyone. How can You say, 'You will be made free'?

Jesus answered them, "Most assuredly, I say to you, whoever commits sin is a slave of sin. And a slave does not abide in the house forever, but a son abides forever. Therefore if the Son makes you free, you shall be free indeed."

If you are a sinner, you can't break free by your own strength. If you are saved and struggling with sin, then you need to get delivered. It is nothing like being free, free from all sin and shame. I wouldn't trade this way of living for anything in the world. You too can have this everlasting salvation and joy that I have. It will work for you if you work it.

I found out I couldn't just know the word and not do the word. I had to learn to live by the word of God. Psalm 119:105New International Version (NIV) "Your word is a lamp for my feet, a light on my path."

Striving for Perfection

In closing, I would like to say that I am not perfect, but I do strive for perfection (restoration). God is not through with me yet. I am facing some things in my life right now that I never had to face before. Maybe that will be in my next book. When I walk out of this thing victoriously, and I know I will, I will put it in a book if the Lord says so! I can speak it with confidence because I already know I have the victory. I just have to walk it out.

Philippians 1:6 New King James Version (NKJV)

"Being confident of this very thing, that He who has begun a good work in you will complete it until the day of Jesus Christ;"

Don't give up and don't give in. Hold on and stay in the race and you will be the winner.

Ecclesiastes 9:11 New King James Version (NKJV)

"I returned and saw under the sun that—The race is not to the swift, Nor the battle to the strong, Nor bread to the wise, Nor riches to men of understanding, Nor favor to men of skill; But time and chance happen to them all."

My Teacher

My Lord has taught me how to run to Him in times of trouble, heartache, disappointment and fear. I have learned to run to Him and find help for any situation or circumstance I am facing. No matter what, I now know I don't have to run away from Him and be all alone trying to solve my problem.

Running from the Lord and trying to run from my problems is what I used to do by chasing the rock (as they used to call it on the streets), but not anymore. Now I run **"TO THE ROCK"** (not the Cocaine rock) that is higher than I (Psalms 61:2b New King James Version "Lead me to the rock that is higher than I"). Many people are chasing the rock cocaine in a big way. I thought I couldn't live a day without it. It tried to fool me, but I know the truth now. **His name is Jesus, the solid Rock!**

One day during a trial, instead of staying in it and doing what I needed to do even if it meant changing and humbling myself, I was going to quit and leave. Suddenly, the Lord told me to stop running, turn around and look the enemy in the face. By doing so, God showed me where I needed to change. I know now, I can advance in adversity.

God is so awesome! You know it's like Pastor Gloria said "God is not going to remove the liquor stores, but He will transform and deliver you so you can drive on by."

Stand Fast!

Galatians 5:1 New King James Version(NKJV)

"Stand fast therefore in the liberty by which Christ has made us free, and do not be entangled again with a yoke of bondage."

I am Free! I am free on the inside and free on the outside, I am free to Worship Him. I am free to praise Him. I am free to Love Him and serve Him. I am no longer bound, there are no more chains binding me. Speaking of bondage, I have even learned to identify it a lot of times. There are times when I notice myself acting and feeling funny, strange or different, and I know something is wrong. First I try to deal with it on m own, but if I don't get it off of me, I don't waddle in it. I have to go to someone, touch and agree in prayer and get delivered. Don't ever be ashamed. Find someone to help you!

Keys to my Success!

I contribute my success, of course, to the Lord saving me, delivering me, and setting me free by the blood of the lamb. He has been a wonderful counselor to me!

I learned how to pray. I learned how to listen. I learned how to walk in obedience. I stayed in my word and I was knowledgeable of the fact I needed to be a doer of the word and not just a hearer only. Put all of this together and you will be able to make it just like I did. No one is any better than I am and I am no better than you are. If God can change me, I know He can change you. I know the enemy is still binding people up like he did me and I am on a mission to expose him. As long as breath remains in a person's body, there is hope for that individual. I don't care how long it takes!

The devil is a liar and the truth is not in him. Don't believe him, he is a defeated foe, and greater is He that is in me (you) than he that is in the world (if you are saved). I used to quote that as a child but since I have lived it, I know, that I know, that I know, it is the truth! There is no situation too hard for the Lord. He is the Lord Almighty. He is the King of Kings and the Lord of Lords!

There's no other like Him in the entire universe. What He has done for me He wants to do for you, and He is willing to do it for you right now! He is waiting on you to just say YES!

Prayer

Prayer is a must because it is my (our) communication with the Lord. I must pray to stay connected and in communion with Him. I don't allow this world to dictate to me when and where I can and cannot pray. There are many times I have to pray silently. If you are told you can't pray in the classroom, YES YOU CAN! Wherever prayer is prohibited, pray all the more, just pray silently! The bible tells us to "Pray without ceasing." (1 Thessalonians 5:17 King James Version)

Study the Word of God

In the beginning I was studying for four hours a day during the week. By doing so it made a tremendous difference in my life. I know many of you may not be able to study for four hours a day. But, whatever time you can devote, it is needed on a daily basis. You should pray for an increase because the Bible is your Soul Food. In the Bible is everything you need to help you make it. It is packed with a wealth of wisdom and knowledge. Besides, if you are going to serve God, you need to know all about Him. You must read your bible, study your Bible, and begin to do what it encourages you do to.

2 Timothy 2:15 King James Version (KJV)

"Study to shew thyself approved unto God, a workman that needeth not to be ashamed, righty dividing the word of truth."

Do the Word

The Bible says to be a doer of the word and not just a hearer only, so I had to learn how to apply the word of God to my life. You can look at it as a math problem. In algebra, if you are given a problem to solve, you can work the problem and come up with an answer at the end, but when you look up the answer you find it is wrong. That is the way it is with life. Many of us have problems and we find a solution for that problem, but in the end, many times the answer we find is wrong. That is why many are incarcerated, on drugs, etc. They worked the problem out the wrong way and came up with the wrong answer and it didn't profit them anything. When we acknowledge God and He shows us the right way to work the problem, the answer is always correct. I don't know about you, but I am feed up with always trying to solve my problems, only to find I didn't accomplish anything.

Proverbs 3:6 New King James Version (NKJV) "In all your ways acknowledge Him, and He shall direct your paths."

Stayed Connected

I stay connected to Christ through reading my word, praying, and going to church on the days we have set aside. I abide with Christ and He abides with me:

John 15:4-6 New Living Translation (NLT)

"Remain in me, and I will remain in you. For a branch cannot produce fruit if it is severed from the vine, and you cannot be fruitful unless you remain in me. Yes, I am the vine; you are the branches. Those who remain in me, and I in them, will produce much fruit. For apart from me you can do nothing. Anyone who does not remain in me is thrown away like a useless branch and withers. Such branches are gathered into a pile to be burned."

Speak the Word

I learned I needed to speak the word of God over my family in any and all situations. Here are a few scriptures I quoted practically daily in the beginning. I call them my "Sustaining Scriptures."

Romans 8:1New King James Version (NKJV)

"There is therefore now no condemnation to those who are in Christ Jesus, who do not walk according to the flesh, but according to the Spirit."

Romans 8:28 New King James Version (NKJV)

"And we know that all things work together for good to those who love God, to those who are the called according to His purpose."

Philippians 4:13New King James Version (NKJV)

"I can do all things through Christ who strengthens me."

1 John 4:4New King James Version (NKJV)

"You are of God, little children, and have overcome them, because He who is in you is greater than he who is in the world."

Isaiah 54:17 New King James Version (NKJV)

"No weapon formed against you shall prosper, And every tongue which rises against you in judgment You shall condemn. This is the heritage of the servants of the LORD, And their righteousness is from Me," Says the LORD.

Philippians 1:6 New King James Version (NKJV)

"being confident of this very thing, that He who has begun a good work in you will complete it until the day of Jesus Christ;"

Philippians 2:12b New International Version (NIV)

"Continue to work out your salvation with fear and trembling"

Hebrews 4:15-16 New International Version (NIV)

"For we do not have a high priest who is unable to empathize with our weaknesses, but we have one who has been tempted in every way, just as we are— yet he didn't sin. Let us then approach God's throne of grace with confidence, so that we may receive mercy and find grace to help us in our time of need."

Proverbs 3:5 New International Version (NIV)

"Trust in the LORD with all your heart and lean not on your own understanding"

Romans 12:2 New International Version (NIV)

"Do not conform to the pattern of this world, but be transformed by the renewing of your mind. Then you will be able to test and approve what God's will is—his good, pleasing and perfect will."

Isaiah 1:18 New King James Version (NKJV)

"Come now, and let us reason together," Says the LORD, " Though your sins are like scarlet, They shall be as white as snow; Though they are red like crimson, They shall be as wool."

Miracle Baby

I would like to take this time and elaborate on my daughter Shishonna Grace. I call her my miracle baby because God truly blessed her in my womb. According to the Organization of Teratology Information Services (OTIS), when a woman uses illegal drugs, smokes or drinks during her pregnancy, all of these substances crosses the placenta and enters the baby's body. Cocaine remains in the baby's body much longer than the adult. In most cases these are some of the things that happen to the baby:

Birth weight is affected, developmental delay, learning problems, behavioral problems, birth defects, small heads, growth restrictions and learning difficulties. Shishonna Grace didn't have any of these things happen to her. Actually she was blessed to be quite the opposite. Praise God!

You have to admit, there is no way medically speaking that a woman can conceive a child and have the lack of nutrition that I had, smoked cigarettes, weed and cocaine. Lighting the cocaine with fire from newspapers, rum, rubbing alcohol, butane lighters and propane. Smoking cocaine out of glass pipes and old TV antennas. There is no way, naturally speaking she should be here, healthy, smart, gifted, and beautiful. It is medically impossible for her not to have some type of disorder physically and/or mentally.

As we know, all of her organs are functioning properly and she has given birth to three healthy, beautiful boys. I wouldn't encourage anyone to do as I did and expect the same outcome, but I am encouraging you to believe in MIRACLES!

I must say Shishonna does struggle with not knowing who her father is and there is no way I can tell her who he is because I do not know. The man I thought was her father was tested a few years ago and it was concluded he wasn't the father. I know it is heart wrenching for her not to know her biological father, but I always try to encourage her to be grateful that she knows God, her heavenly father, and my husband who has been here for her since she was a little girl. It works for many days, but there are some days the facts tend to bring her down. Because I serve an awesome God, I know He will see her through, because He saw fit for her to be here! My Miracle Baby!

New Life

I like living this kind of life! I am living the best life. I served the devil well and I got nothing in return except for degradation, heartache, disappointment, pain, shame and separation from God. Now, the best is yet to come! Every day is a blessed day in the Lord. I do rejoice and be glad in it. I have learned to count my blessing one by one and focus on them and not my troubles. As long as I live, I will have problems and troubles from time to time, but God will see me through them all.

In my sickness, I didn't know living life the way it is supposed to be, could be so enjoyable, rewarding and exciting, but it really is. You can't see it when you are living in darkness. To my amazement, I found it is really better to serve the Lord and I love it. I will never go back to serving the enemy because he has nothing to offer me. By living a life of sin and serving him, I have absolutely nothing to gain but heartache and pain. Now I must admit, while serving the Lord everyday has not been a happy day. I have had some disappointments and some weary days, but I have the comforter to see me through. In other words, as long as we live we are all going to have to go through trials and tribulations, but I would much rather go through them with the Lord on my side than without Him!

Power of Forgiveness

To know the power of forgiveness and walk in it is a beautiful thing. I used to hold myself as well as others captive by not forgiving. I remember one day when I read in:

Matthew 6:15 New International Version (NIV)

"But if you do not forgive others their sins, your Father will not forgive your sins."

I was in awe for so long. I was asking God to forgive me and believed I was being forgiven until I read this scripture. Now I know, I have to live my life walking in forgiveness as well as continue to ask for forgiveness. We must forgive in order to be forgiven!

Heart's Desire

My heart's desire is to see all of God's children delivered and set free by the blood of the lamb. If He delivered me, He can deliver anyone. I know if He can bless my baby in the womb, protect her from all of the terrible things I was doing and putting in my body, I know He can do anything but Fail! He is a Miracle Worker!

2 Timothy 1:7 New International Version (TNIV)

"For the Spirit God gave us does not make us timid, but gives us power, love and self-discipline."

Psalm 1:1-3King James Version (KJV) Seek wise counsel:

"Blessed is the man that walketh not in the counsel of the ungodly, nor standeth in the way of sinners, nor sitteth in the seat of the scornful. But his delight is in the law of the LORD; and in his law doth he meditate day and night. And he shall be like a tree planted by the rivers of water, that bringeth forth his fruit in his season; his leaf also shall not wither; and whatsoever he doeth shall prosper."

I shall not be moved! People of all ages are bound and having trouble. I wanted to write this book and make it plan so all readers can be blessed.

SALVATION

"The thief's purpose is to steal and kill and destroy. My purpose is to give them a rich and satisfying life." John 10:10 New Living Translation (NLT)

"For God so loved the world that he gave his one and only Son, that whoever believes in him shall not perish but have eternal life." John 3:16 New Living Translation (NLT)

"For I know the plans I have for you," declares the Lord, "plans to prosper you and not to harm you, plans to give you hope and a future" Jeremiah 29:11 New International Version (NIV).

Now I encourage you to pray this prayer of salvation according to: ***Romans 10:9-10 New King James Version*** (NKJV)

"that if you confess with your mouth the Lord Jesus and believe in your heart that God has raised Him from the dead, you will be saved. For with the heart one believes unto righteousness, and with the mouth confession is made unto salvation."

Dear Lord,
I come before you right now in the name of Jesus confessing that I have sinned against you.
Lord I believe you sent your only Son, to die on the cross, shed his blood and rose from the dead for my sins. I believe Jesus is the Son of God.
Jesus, I ask that you would forgive me of all of my sins, known and unknown and cleanse me of all unrighteousness. Everything that is not pleasing to you, Lord I ask you to forgive me.
Lord Jesus, I ask you to search the four corners of my heart and cast out everything that is not like you.
Lord, I confess that apart from you I can do nothing; I ask that you would live in me and I in you. Please renew a right spirit in me.
Lord, I ask that you would heal me, cleanse me, and deliver me from the chains that have me bound. Set me free by the blood of the lamb.
Lord Jesus, I ask you to come into my heart and fill me with your precious Holy Spirit.
Father I thank you because I believe by faith my sins are forgiven and I am saved.
Thank you Jesus.
Amen

Congratulations and welcome to the beginning of a new and exciting life! Praise God! Praise God! Praise God! Now you are saved!!! Shout Hallelujah! Hallelujah! Hallelujah!!! Now go and confess your salvation to three or more people

The angels in heaven are rejoicing and so am I!

Church Home

Again, I advise you to pray for a good church home. When you are sure that is where God wants you to be, stay there and don't leave until He tells you to.

Church folks will be church folks. Everybody in the church is not saved and everybody in the church who is saved is not fully delivered. There may be some mess in the church or shall I say some messy people in the church. If you happen to encounter them, walk in love or walk the other way and keep your salvation and "Stay in Church. Don't let the devil run you off of your post." When I first started going back to church, I saw a lot of things that weren't right in my eyes and I saw things in my own life that weren't right. As I stayed and grew a little, I came to find we are all just people in need of help in one way or another. You may not need to change in the same area that I need to change, but you need change too. We all do! I tell people,

The enemy will use people in the church to discourage you and cause you to back up and not go anymore. Don't back down and while you are going to church Sunday after Sunday, it is best that you learn something. Don't just go to say that you are going. While you are going, you should be growing and if you are not growing then something is definitely wrong and you need to seek the Lord about it.

Holy Spirit

I remember going to church and always hearing people talk about the Holy Spirit. I wanted to know more about this person. I searched my Bible to learn all I could. Then one day I heard someone talking about The Television Minister, Benny Hinn and that he had written a book called *Good Morning Holy Spirit*. I had to get the book and read it. When I first starting reading it I could hardly put it down. I would encourage everyone to read this book. I was so enlightened. It gave me a good understanding of who the Holy Spirit is and what his position is. After reading the book, I prayed and ask the Holy Spirit to work with me and train me to know when He was speaking to me. He didn't waste any time. I tell you the truth, he is already speaking to many of you but you just don't know who He is. Many times people will refer to Him as "something told me". That something is the Holy Spirit. His job is to lead, guide, warn and protect.

I told my husband that I had told the Holy Ghost to work with me and teach me so if he thought I was acting strange he would know why. One day we were in the car getting ready to leave. I heard this voice say, "Go back in the house in the kitchen." So I told my husband to wait, I needed to go back in the house. He asked me, "For what?" I told him, "I don't know I just have to go back in the house!" He said, "Oh Yes" sarcastically, "I know the Holy Ghost told you." As he put the car in park, I jumped out and ran back into the house. I went into the kitchen and I didn't see anything wrong. I looked around and the lights were off, the back door was locked and the stove was off. I asked, "What Holy Spirit? What did you have me come back in here for?" He didn't say a word, so I turned around and started to head back to the front door. As I turned around that is when I saw what he was trying to show me. I was about to forget something that I needed to take with me.

I could go on and on about the Holy Spirit. But, instead I encourage you to get the book and read it for yourself. Pray about it and allow God to reveal to you who He is, and how He communicates with us on a daily basis. I know now it was the Holy Spirit who warned me to get out of the house that night when I was using drugs. If I didn't leave I probably would have been shot in the head. They showed me where the bullet hit the wall as the man fired rounds in the house. I sat in shock because where the hole in the wall was, is the same spot where I was standing. Many, many times I can tell you before and after my deliverance that he has spoken to me to warn me.

He has helped me find things I couldn't find and the list goes on and on. So don't forget to get to know Him because He is who we communicate with on a daily basis. Jesus said I wouldn't leave you comfortless. "However, when He, the Spirit of truth, has come, He will guide you into all truth; for He will not speak on His own authority, but whatever He hears He will speak; and He will tell you things to come (John 16:13 New King James Version).

What the enemy meant for my harm the Lord has turned it around for my good. I am on a mission to help set the captive free!

My Accomplishments:

I have maintained my **SALVATION** for 24+ years.

I managed to remain in my **MARRIAGE** for 35+years.

For 24+ years I have managed to raise my two children and take care of our home like the Proverb 31 woman. Remained **FAITHFUL** to my husband, and maintained my integrity and sobriety.

For 20+ years I have remained on my job and in the same church.

In July 1993, I founded "Daughters of Destiny Women's Ministry" at Holiness Church of Deliverance in Hopkinsville, KY.

I have learned how to be a good grandmother and mother-in-law.

I have been a member of "Rhema Word Jail Ministry" for over 14 years.

I have published my first book.

My greatest accomplishment of all is I have been a kingdom builder since 1987.

I have great **Success** because I am a Child of the King!

Luke 9:25 New King James Version (NKJV)

"For what profit is it to a man if he gains the whole world, and is himself destroyed or lost?"

I NEVER WOULD HAVE MADE IT WITHOUT THE LORD JESUS CHRIST!

God is a good God! He is a Deliverer! He is a Restorer! He is my All and ALL!

I AM A **LIVING** EXAMPLE OF THE WORD OF GOD!

I pray you are encouraged, inspired, enlightened and blessed!

JESUS LOVES YOU, AND SO DO I!

"I praise you because I am fearfully and wonderfully made; your works are wonderful, I know that full well."(Psalms 139:14 New International Version)

Thank You Lord!

Victory is Mines!

Victory Can Be Yours Also!

Psalms 1:1-3 New King James Version (NKJV)

"Blessed is the man who walks not in the counsel of the ungodly, nor stands in the path of sinners, nor sits in the seat of the scornful; but his delight is in the law of the Lord, and in his law he meditates day and night. He shall be like a tree planted by the rivers of water, that brings forth its fruit in its season, whose leaf also shall not wither; and whatever he does shall prosper."

In closing I would like to say, for the most part I had a wonderful childhood. My family, I would not trade them for the world. It was the sin that ultimately destroyed my life. It was God who gave it back. I have a second chance and I am grateful. Everyone who caused me harm I have forgiven. Every rapist, every one has been forgiven. I realize sick people do sick things, and they need to be delivered. Therefore I prayed for them. There were things that I did that were not mentioned and I too had to ask for forgiveness.

After all of the drugs I took, and many were not mentioned, I have a healthy body. My mind is good and my lungs are too. God has been merciful to me and I thank Him continuously for His kindness. My heart and prayers go out to all who are bound. I cried sorely over all who did not make it, often times wondering, "Why me Lord!" I know my life was spared for a reason. I have a work to do for the Lord. My life is not my own.

Thank you for hearing my story.

It's the Truth!

May God bless you!

Mom and Dad

5th Grade

Sisters in 1973

Newlyweds

Mom and Girls - 2005

The Jackson Family

4-24-12 1 of 1

Sha Jackson shared her story with the hope that it will help others. She credits her parent's unwavering support and unconditional love during what seemed to be her darkest days.

Visit my website at:
shajacksonministries.vpweb.com